Recollections of
Waterloo Lutheran University
1960–1973

Happy memories !
Dorothy

Recollections of
Waterloo Lutheran University
1960–1973

Flora Roy

Wilfrid Laurier University Press

[WLU]

We acknowledge the financial support and services in kind of the Alumni Association, Bookstore, Development Office, Special Initiatives Funding, and University Advancement of Wilfrid Laurier University. We acknowledge the financial support of the Government of Canada through the Book Publishing Industry Development Program for our publishing activities.

Library and Archives Canada Cataloguing in Publication

Roy, Flora
    Recollections of Waterloo Lutheran University 1960–1973 / Flora Roy.

Sequel to: Recollections of Waterloo College.
ISBN-13: 978-0-88920-502-4
ISBN-10: 0-88920-502-7

    1. Roy, Flora. 2. Waterloo Lutheran University—History.
3. College teachers—Ontario—Waterloo—Biography. 4. Waterloo
Lutheran University—Faculty—Biography. I. Title.

LE3.W48R69 2006   378.713'45092   C2006-905072-4

© 2006 Flora Roy

Cover and text design by P.J. Woodland. The front-cover photograph shows a stained-glass window in the Waterloo Lutheran Seminary at Wilfrid Laurier University. Back-cover photograph courtesy of the *Record*.

Every reasonable effort has been made to acquire permission for copyright material used in this text, and to acknowledge all such indebtedness accurately. Any errors and omissions called to the publisher's attention will be corrected in future printings.

Printed in Canada

Contents

Preface / vii

Acknowledgements / ix

Chronology / x

Preface

A CURRENT READER OF THIS BOOK may be excused for asking a few background questions.

1. *What was the origin of the short-lived Waterloo Lutheran University?* It was founded in 1960, having been developed out of Waterloo College. It included an academic component and a seminary, the latter largely devoted to the training of those who would become Lutheran pastors.

2. *What does Lutheran mean?* Lutheranism was a religious movement in Europe that began in the sixteenth century and was made up of the followers of Martin Luther. He was one of many reformers who objected to perceived weaknesses in the Church of Rome. Lutheranism became the official religion in a number of German states, in Scandinavia, and elsewhere through migration and missionary efforts. Later, followers joined less as a matter of state and more as a matter of individual conscience.

    The first Lutheran synod in North America was formed in 1748. In time, many American Lutheran groups developed, later merging into three main groups. The one under which Waterloo College had operated became part of the United Lutheran Church in America (ULCA), formed in 1962. That changed in 1986 when the Evangelical Lutheran Synod in Canada was formed to operate independently, though still connected to the ULCA.

The change had little to do with Waterloo Lutheran University, which by that time had become the provincially sponsored body, Wilfrid Laurier University.

3. *To what extent was Waterloo Lutheran University affected by the religious affiliation?* My research leads me to conclude that the effect was of little significance, if it existed at all. Faculty and staff represented the Waterloo community as a whole. For instance, along with Lutherans and others, we had Muslim students and faculty, and for a time we had more Jewish and Roman Catholic students than Lutherans. Lutherans on campus received no special privileges.

4. *Was the seminary a part of Waterloo Lutheran University?* A search of financial statements in minutes of annual meetings of the synod reveals that in 1961, during the first years of the university, the seminary was allotted 0.8 percent of the budget. In 1973, at the end, the figure was 0.7 percent. It is not my intent here to discover how the seminary paid its bills, but I suspect that donations helped considerably. I did learn of one discreet loan from an academic source, but it is obvious that the seminarians posed a minimal cost to the institution.

5. *Why did Waterloo Lutheran University end?* You will have to read the book to find out.

Acknowledgements

Dr. Margaret Evans, a paragon of editors

Joan Mitchell, a patient and ever-helpful archivist

Charlotte Cox, interpreter and scribe

Dr. Paul Tiessen, champion

And to all donors, financial and otherwise, without whom this book would not have been possible.

The royalties from the sale of this book will fund scholarships.

Chronology

1911 The Evangelical Lutheran Seminary of Canada opens.

1914 Facilities for pre-theological education are established, with courses leading to senior matriculation given by Waterloo College School.

1924 Waterloo College of Arts is established. It provides a four-year program of post-secondary education.

1925 The Faculty of Arts, under the name Waterloo College, is affiliated with the University of Western Ontario. The college offers honours degrees in the arts. (In 1927 there were 87 students.)

1960 Affiliation with Western ends with the college's revised charter, which changes the name of the institution to Waterloo Lutheran University.

1973 On November 1, Waterloo Lutheran University becomes Wilfrid Laurier University, with a student enrolment of 2,299.

CHAPTER I

Finances

I AM GOING TO WRITE ABOUT what I recall of the short life of Waterloo Lutheran University (1960–1973), and I will probably, consciously or unconsciously, leave the impression that those of us involved in that institution's growth were remarkably bright, creative, and dedicated, while ignoring the reality that we were perhaps just lucky. We were working in an especially propitious economic era. Expanding job opportunities, abundant credit, new markets, and increasing amounts of disposable income in the hands of the employed—all of these factors gave us an optimism that allowed us to act without second thoughts and allowed us both to make mistakes and to pull off considerable triumphs.

Not that Waterloo Lutheran University itself had any money—that is, in comparison to the rest of the new Ontario universities that burgeoned in that time of fresh beginnings, or in relation to the income and endowments of the older schools, which considered themselves threatened by the largesse of the province to their younger relations. I am not going to research the financial records; a historian or graduate student can do that. My intention is to convey what it felt like to work for growth and improvement, knowing that we had to stay within a very close budget.

The historian can check the official records of income and expenditure, but those of us who had the responsibility of spending the money will always recall a charming little figure in a fashionable black suit and heels, sitting behind a huge book, which she always consulted when we came to her office with requests for funds. I can thankfully recall that I was never refused, but I also recall the preceding hours of planning arguments and weighing the advantages and disadvantages of a certain expenditure. I will mention some of my requests in connection with other topics, but here I will say briefly that once I had to ask her for the phenomenal short-term insurance premium necessary to protect a valuable art collection that we hoped to invite on campus. Tamara Giesbrecht just smiled and nodded her blond head. I don't know where she found the money, but it was worth it.

I will never be able to name all the people at Waterloo Lutheran University who kept us afloat, but while I am recalling Miss Giesbrecht, let me add that a handful of dedicated women—accountants, secretaries, cooks, et al.—did as much as faculty and administration, and perhaps more. For instance, when we had to supply budgeted expense accounts for departments, the woman responsible for them insisted on seeing actual receipts to cover all spending before we could have any further advances. When we became a provincial university, there was less interest in saving money, and the close supervision of expenditure was given up. I was told that my successor as department head lamely explained an LCBO (Liquor Control Board of Ontario) receipt as having something to do with the library, and I believe he got away with it.

Where did the money come from? Again I leave it to the historian to look in the records and calculate the relative contributions from at least five sources: the federal government, the Canadian Mortgage and Housing Office (National Housing Act), the Lutheran Church and individual or corporate sponsors, summer school and extension enrolments, and intramural tuition fees and other charges upon the students.

The federal government grants were crucial. Were they one of the results of the 1951 report of the Massey Commission (the Royal Commission on National Developments in the Arts, Letters, and Sciences)? I recall the general enthusiasm at the time for government encouragement of the non-commercial aspects of national life, and the sprouting of various councils to give awards to promising students, artists, and musicians. Generally it was all regarded as a good thing, and I don't recall any particular grumbling or worrying about the sources of the money or about deficits.

We were able to make use of another federal initiative in order to provide the modern (albeit cheap) buildings we needed partly for practical reasons, but also so that skeptics could view from the street what was soon going to look like a university, as more and more buildings were added between King and Albert streets, ousting the dairy farm and the cider mill.

While we were still Waterloo College, Dr. Herman Overgaard had heard that McMaster University was appealing directly to the federal government for funds. He suggested that the Waterloo College Board send an intermediary to find out if we could tap into the same source. The only problem was that the recipient institution would have to match the federal grant; where could we find that kind of money?

Dr. Overgaard had another inspiration. Could we get a grant under the National Housing Act for the student residences we were about to build, and use that money to match the federal grant from the first source? (I append his letter to Senator Walker, and Mrs. Walker's reply, which confirms Dr. Overgaard's recollections of the original approach.) As the letters indicate, the flurry of building on university campuses was to be a stimulation to the economy, but without the optimism of the "golden years," from 1960 to 1973, the funds would never have been forthcoming.

Letter One

March 5, 1997
298 Lourdes Crescent
Waterloo, Ontario
N3L 1P5

Senator David Walker
65 Glen Edyth Drive
Toronto, Ontario
M4V 2V8

Dear Senator Walker:

Some of my colleagues are engaged in a project of writing the history of our University, Wilfrid Laurier University, formerly called Waterloo Lutheran University. As I am the oldest living faculty member still around, my colleagues have asked me to furnish them with some documentation concerning the furnishing of funds by your Government in 1959–60 to universities in Canada for the construction of buildings for Arts facilities. Accordingly I am briefly noting below some comments that I recall that you made when you visited our campus in Waterloo in 1960 to dedicate the new Girls' Residence and the new Theatre-Auditorium building.

You may recall that in 1959 I sent you a letter in your capacity as Minister of Public Works, and a copy to the Prime Minister, explaining that because of the explosion in university enrolment across Canada, university facilities were woefully inadequate. I indicated that, in my opinion, unemployment was becoming such a problem that by that winter I expected that it would reach at least nine percent—which was considered to be a very high figure at that time. However, in view of the fact that most Canadian universities had at least one building on the drawing board, ready for construction, with several more to follow, I suggested that your Government amend the National Housing Act to permit the universities to borrow funds, much like individuals, at a preferred rate of $5\frac{1}{4}\%$ for forty years. I believed that such action would stimulate Canada's construction industry and increase employment through the multiplier effect. I also noted in my letter that this change had already been made in the US via the Federal Housing Act. Accordingly, your Government brought in legislation that fall offering funds to Canadian universities at $5\frac{1}{8}$ percent. The result was a flurry of construction by universities all across the country.

At the dedication ceremonies, you informed me that you had not given any thought to this change in the NHA until you received my letter. In your dedication speech on our campus, you stated that all the other Canadian universities owed our University a vote of thanks for coming up with the suggestion.

If you concur in the above or wish to make corrections, please do so and append your signature below. Thank you very much for your kind assistance in this matter.

Yours sincerely,

Herman Overgaard	*David J. Walker*
Professor Emeritus of	(per Elizabeth J. Walker)
International Business	To the best of my recollection
School of Business	the above information is correct
Wilfrid Laurier University	

Signed: *Senator David Walker*

Letter Two

March 25, 1997
65 Glen Edyth Drive
Toronto, Ontario
M4V 2V8

Professor Herman Overgaard
298 Lourdes Crescent
Waterloo, Ontario
N2L 1P5

Dear Professor Overgaard:

May I write you, on behalf of my late husband Senator David Walker who passed away on Sept. 22/95.

Thank you for your kind letter to Dave, in reference to the needs of Wilfrid Laurier University, which I believe at that time was known as Waterloo Lutheran University in 1959.

I have taken the liberty of signing Dave's name, after referring to his notes on the subject.

With all good wishes.

Sincerely,
Elizabeth J. Walker
(Mrs. David J. Walker)

The sharp reader may have detected something a little unusual in the successful attempt to use one federal grant to obtain another from a different department, but it took the authorities several years to notice the anomaly and that gave us time to get our building program underway. (Dr. Overgaard had also alerted a couple of other university presidents, friends of his, to the financial manoeuvre I have just described, urging them to make use of it quickly for obvious reasons. I do not know if they followed his hint. Neither university was in Ontario.)

Dr. Overgaard mentions in his letter to Senator Walker the new girls' residence (the word "girl" carried no stigma then) and the theatre-auditorium, but soon we had an athletic complex, a dining hall, and more residences. I'll leave it to a researcher to find out how many of our new buildings were funded by government-backed loans, but we can rest on the assertion that without that backing, we could not have come so far and so fast by the end of our golden era in 1973.

Not only were we taking money, we were also making it. Just as soon as possible after we received our charter, Dean Schaus and Professor Clark were planning our summer school and extension outreach. Our good relations with the University of Western Ontario made the allocations of areas for extension centres easy and peaceable, and there was no limit to what we could offer on campus, except for hiring enough suitable faculty.

Our success came partly from our attempts to offer a wide range of courses (the University of Toronto external program was rather limited, for instance) and to maintain the standards we set in intramural classes. I must add that the Ontario government had aided the universities by insisting that public school teachers should attain at least a bachelor of arts degree—not a bachelor of education. As a result, for a number of years our external courses were crowded with teachers.

I might mention here a special new program in which we accepted certain gifted grade twelve graduates into our summer school courses. If they were successful—and if they wished—they could register in our first-year program, making up the necessary extra credits along the way. Several of our most interesting honours students came to us by this route. Others went back to high school to get the usual grade twelve credits, but with a new sense of what was meant by higher education. We made no money from government funds for these grade twelve students because their status was irregular, but we raised the intellectual level of our student body with those who stayed in our programs.

Further funds to support Waterloo Lutheran University came from the usual charges for tuition, which we had to keep low, because before long, with all the new Ontario universities in the game, there was competition to attract students. We refused to compromise on standards for graduation, though we had ways of attracting students to enter. For instance, students could take three courses at an advanced level to find out if they could handle academic material. I believe that a second try was allowed, too. I wonder if we have a record of those who went on to professional careers from our trial enrolment. The students had a saying that Waterloo Lutheran University was easy to get into, but very hard to get out of.

How much did the Lutheran Church contribute? Not as much as the university would have wished, I suspect. A church ladies' auxiliary was helpful. (They even provided a silver service for university "teas.") There were bequests and donations, but not enough to keep the roof up when the bad days came.

As might be expected, our income from summer school and extension fell as more and more teachers obtained their degrees, and fewer new ones appeared, because they were required to get degrees before their teacher training. The university administration blamed the head of our extension school for the decline, and hired replacements, thus initiating a period of academic in-fighting that brought little credit to anyone except Professor Clark, the initiator of our extension program, who retained the respect and affection of students and faculty, and carried the severe wounds of the fray with dignity. But our income was undoubtedly lessened.

The real blow came when the federal government started handing over to the provinces the funds that the universities had formerly received directly. Because we were independent, the Ontario government cut our grant to half of that given to each provincial university. Though a group of Lutherans made a brave attempt to show that the university could continue to be financially viable on its own, it was clear that to keep up the standards we had achieved, more provincial funding would be essential. The only solution was to give up the church affiliation and become a provincial university. As one of our publicity brochures puts it, "Waterloo Lutheran University achieve[d] full provincial status under the new name of Wilfrid Laurier University." Recently I heard a Lutheran say with regret and, I think, some shame, "We sold the university," which pretty well states the situation. But there was no alternative. I was on the platform on the occasion when the banner reading "Waterloo Lutheran University" was changed to "Wilfrid Laurier University." It was not my happiest occasion. Even an atheist might have wondered if academic life would be better under a provincial government than under a church. At least the church doesn't change directions every time there is an election.

There are some broader ironies. The astute Dr. Potter, who had had much to do with keeping Waterloo College afloat, once said within my hearing, "Never name a university after a person. The time may come when you will be sorry." He was thinking of the many turns of fashion—or of the revelations—that can change a reputation, but in this instance we can wonder at the choice of a French-Canadian name for an institution that someday may find itself in the Rest of Canada, while Sir Wilfrid's home province of Quebec goes its own way. One of the administrators responsible for the new name had studied at Laval and may have felt that honouring Laurier in Ontario might help to hold Canada together. One might add that the new name had the same initials as the old, so that anything marked WLU could still be used by the new regime. The new Wilfrid Laurier University, however, would not be bankrupt now that it had its rightful share of provincial funding.

CHAPTER II

University Government

———— ❧ ————

How should a university be governed? In the early eleventh century, the University of Bologna was run by the students who elected their own governors. The University of Paris, consolidated towards the end of the twelfth century, was ruled largely by the teachers. But behind the governors, there was usually a final power; in the early history of Western European learning, it was usually the church, with more or less attention from the court. Later, with a new public interest in higher education expressed through city corporations, groups with special concerns (such as science), or wealthy founders, more parties claimed some voice in directing the institutions they supported. Ideally, in our time taxpayers will even be able to request some share of the power that once was exercised in education by bishops or the agents of emperors or kings.

In the old Waterloo College, the head of the Department of Romance Languages was a certain Don Evans, who had served as a liaison officer between the Canadian and French armies in the First World War. There, and in other experiences of real life, he had acquired wisdom. He once remarked to me, not in relation to any campus crisis, but as a useful generalization, "There never is enough power to go around." In subsequent years I have noted the deep truth of that adage, which I have no doubt was as true in classical Rome and in seventeenth-century France as it was on the Waterloo

College campus. Every attempt to share power equably and equally, it seems, ends in a power struggle.

Waterloo Lutheran University could not hope to be spared the inherent problems in any organization, but which to observers of academe seem especially to plague universities. I have been told that Woodrow Wilson, when he exchanged the presidency of Princeton University for the national political field, remarked, "I learned my politics among professionals. Now I am among amateurs." The story of our golden years, from 1960 to 1973, was a story of increasing political strains, culminating in the hiring by the Board of Governors of the Booz Allen Hamilton consulting firm to sort us out. That move resulted in the resignation of the president and the demotion of the dean, leaving the field clear of internecine struggle, with power apparently relegated as much as possible to faceless committees. We came to that end by our own route, but it was an end that most, if not all, universities moved towards in the 1960s. I am not sure that everyone was pleased. At a gathering of members of English departments from all over Canada—sometime in the late 1960s—a very young lecturer interrupted the discussion of weightier matters to register a protest against the trend to rule by committee. "In the old days," he cried, "if I was treated badly, I would punch someone's nose, but now I don't know whose nose to punch." I don't think he knew that he could have sued the individual members of those seemingly abstract committees, as well as the university. When I left the committee, which oversaw promotion and tenure, I gave thanks that no one had found occasion to sue us during my term.

A detailed study of the movement, from the relatively uncluttered administration of Waterloo Lutheran University in 1960 to the carefully layered and branched governance of Wilfrid Laurier University today, would make a good graduate paper, or even an MA thesis. On the surface, the researcher would have to read all the documents available to prepare some sort of chronology; however, it might be more difficult to sniff out the underlying reason for each change: a subtle move to dislodge an opponent, an attempt to unbalance a rival, or a genuine desire to improve fairness and efficiency. The human side of the reforms would be harder to ascertain, but more interesting than minutes of meetings or reports of committees. Both approaches I will leave to a professional. Instead, I propose to outline briefly the administrative structure at Waterloo Lutheran University, and to give my impressions of a few individuals who, for better or worse, made it work, with some reference to the personal dramas that proved our humanity—and our frailty—as we all shared in the competition for power.

The Board of Governors was ostensibly the source of all power, with its chairman the visible sign of its dominance, but there was still some oversight from the American body to which at that time the local synod belonged. As was shown at the time of the "split" from the Associate Faculties (that is to say, the University of Waterloo), the synod, too, had the right to overrule the board.

Academically and administratively, the chancellor was an important symbol, and could prove to be an aid in lobbying for favours from VIPs in government or commerce, or in the professions, but I do not recall any instances of chancellors initiating or pressing for certain policies on campus, though they gave useful advice if asked.

The president of the university was in a position to be overlord of the whole enterprise, which comprised Waterloo University College, the seminary and, in time, a college of the Mennonite Brethren in Winnipeg, which was affiliated with us until the University of Winnipeg came into being and seemed to them to be the obvious body with which to be associated. We had four presidents in the golden years, one of whom, Dr. Villaume, was an example of university president as supreme ruler, but he resigned when he saw a challenge to his primacy from the consultants brought in by the board. (Dr. Villaume had been appointed because Dr. Frye of the American church had recommended him as an administrator with experience and personality to handle the problems that would arise after the division of Waterloo College into two universities.)

I suppose all universities in their beginnings ask a great deal of their first administrators, but I think church-affiliated institutions are especially liable to ask too much of individuals, and finding that the asking is not all in vain, they may heap more responsibility and work on committed men or women. That was certainly true of Waterloo College. In one crisis, when the dean at the time resigned to take a job at the University of Western Ontario (which was having its own crisis), our college appealed to a loyal graduate, Lloyd Schaus. He had served ably as a pastor, especially in wartime Ottawa, where his congregation was swelled by European Lutherans who were in Canada as refugees or as representatives of governments in exile. At last, however, he became free to pursue his first interest, scholarship, and off he went to Columbia to work towards a doctorate in Old Testament studies. When the call came to drop his studies and save the college he complied, and never again did he have a chance to be a private citizen. Schaus took on the duties of dean, and in emergencies of registrar, bursar, student and faculty counsellor—as well as of husband and father—and became to faculty and students the real head of the college, and then of the university. Looking back, it is hard to believe that one man could have done so much. Incidentally, in one of his busiest times his wife was diagnosed with incipient tuberculosis and ordered to take a year's bedrest at home, so that Dean Schaus looked after the children, his wife, and the housekeeping. (Our salaries in those days didn't run to private nurses and expensive housekeepers, and publicly funded home care hadn't been established.)

I recall an occasion that will illustrate how we depended on the dean. One Sunday I was called suddenly to Saskatchewan; a relative was very seriously ill. I arranged quickly for the first flight out—one leaving in the middle of the night—and then called a taxi company to order a car at two o'clock in the morning. Only then did I call the dean. He was kind as always, but brief. Shortly afterwards, he called me back. He and his wife would arrive at a late hour to take me to the airport. I was glad to be able to assure him that transportation was arranged—though I knew that they were proffering their comforting presence, as well as their vehicle. With all the duties that the day would bring, they could ill afford to spend the night on the road, but they didn't hesitate. Over and over, they gave their time and strength for faculty members and students. You can see why we felt that the essence of our university was to be found in our dean. It is no surprise that the all-powerful president, Dr. Villaume, felt challenged by a dean who was even more powerful as a campus personality, and thus when the president felt he must resign, he stipulated that the dean, too, must go. I have no inside knowledge of the battle that ensued between the board, committed to the promise made to the president, and the friends of the dean, who were trying to have the dismissal revoked, but I can append a letter to a board member (courtesy of Dr. Overgaard) that gives some idea of the context. In the meantime, the dean was ill—and though a place was found for him in Religion and Culture, he was never again a well man.

◦◦◦

August 25, 1967
298 Lourdes Crescent
Waterloo, Ontario
N3P 1P5

Dear Herbert,

Something happened here today that I thought you had better know about before the Board of Governors meeting. Henry Endress came to see Lloyd Schaus at his home this afternoon, and from the sounds of things, Henry had received Koerber's letter and was quite upset by it.

After some talk about generalities, Henry enquired in detail about Lloyd's health and Lloyd made it quite plain that he was not out of the woods yet nor would he be for about one month, if then. He told Henry to check it out with two doctors if he didn't believe Lloyd.

Henry then mentioned that he had received a letter from an alumnus—no name mentioned—who had expressed great concern for Lloyd's health and had become "emotional" about it by using the term "critically ill."

Henry warned Lloyd that he had discussed the letter with Harry Greb and that it would not be discussed at the Full Board meeting. One of the reasons Henry gave was that when a minister leaves his congregation, he has nothing further to do with the congregation, and so it was with Lloyd and Villaume. Upon hearing this Lloyd really tore into Henry and told Henry that most of what Henry was administering now was there because of what Lloyd had done and not Villaume's doing. I guess they had it out hot and heavy for over an hour. Lloyd also pointed out that his demotion had been rail-roaded through the Board and there were several who had not gone along with the motion, contrary to what Greb had told Schaus.

Schaus asked Henry why he was pestering him about the letter instead of contacting its author. Henry's reply was that he had not had time to contact the author, but wanted Lloyd to know there was no hope of any change now. Lloyd said that was o.k., as long as there was a change made now for next year so Lloyd could plan ahead.

In view of Henry's statement that Koerber's letter would not be taken up with the Board, I feel you have a right and that you must request that the letter be read at the Board meeting. If the secretary of the faculty received a letter and did not read it to the faculty there sure would be trouble on the line. I guess the best strategy would be to give notice of your motion when the meeting starts so it will be on the agenda, and then during its discussion you could ask for the letter to be read. If for some reason they refuse to read it, then you could ask permission to read your copy which I asked Koerber to send to you today. Be sure you get Eric Winkler to second the motion, which means you must be certain he is going to be there. Lloyd asked me to write to you and ask you to try to come and see him for a half hour or so before the Board meeting as he cannot travel to see you. He itches something terrible. He told Henry a new administrative position would cure it.

Sincerely,
Herman Overgaard

In the golden years, department heads were more powerful than they have ever been since that time. Though we had been trans-formed into chairmen along the way, many of us still acted as if we were heads, and in our council, which met regularly with the dean, we had what I think was the strongest influence on university policy of all the parts of the administrative structure. We did not confine ourselves to academic matters. In fact, a case of injustice against a colleague in the matter of a Summer School appointment brought us to the board to appeal a ruling by the president, and that finally resulted in the president's resignation. (The Villaume–Little correspondence can be found in the university archives.) After that, our power declined, as parts of the university became schools, with deans of their own, and a Council of Deans replaced the Council of Department Heads to maintain standards and inaugurate creative changes.

That shuffle of power was a pity, because the department heads (chairmen) were closely in touch with their members, and through them there was an opening for participation in university decisions for very humble faculty. Later it became more and more difficult to inaugurate programs unless they were initiated by someone in the new office of Vice-President: Academic or by a dean. I once tried to tell an ambitious young professor how things were done in the golden years, and could see the look of polite incredulity come over his face: I must be mistaken. How could a university run without vice-presidents and deans? I gave up. We were talking mutually incomprehensible languages.

Another powerful body was the Faculty Council that included every academic appointee, and was chaired by the dean. From the beginning, in this council, as in the group of chairmen, opinions were expressed freely. I really do not recall much if any political posturing: holding one's fire against weak arguments to ensure support for oneself later, or attacking just to destabilize a possible rival. The liveliest meeting of the year came when we were turned into a committee to judge the examination records of the students.

A screen was set up, and one by one the students' records appeared. If there was to be any modification of marks, or any bending of rules, it was to be done with the consent of the whole body. It was a very trying several hours, and most people were happy, I think, when the proceedings were transferred to a committee connected to the Registrar's Office, but the process guaranteed fairness, it militated against errors in final reports, and it enabled faculty members to compare their own evaluations against those of their colleagues. For instance, in one of the revolutionary periods we went through (this one may be a little later than the golden years), we had an especially radical professor who was a champion of student power. When his marks appeared on the screen, we saw that two of his students had been given Bs, though the rest of us knew they had spent most of the year off-campus. I knew them quite well and they had informed me proudly they were off to Toronto to audition for *Hair*. I should explain that as a first example of showing full-frontal nudity on stage the production was a bit of a scandal, so I could see why these rebellious young men wanted to be associated with it. But I didn't show my amusement at the idea that obviously they thought they had the means of impressing the casting director. They later reported, crestfallen, that the other competitors came with agents and lawyers, which counted for more than suitability for the nude chorus line, but they added that they so much enjoyed the atmosphere they were going back until the rehearsals were over—as "groupies" of *Hair*, in effect.

When someone pointed out at the meeting that the two no-shows on campus had been assigned what in those days was a high mark, the radical professor said lamely, "Anyone who enrols in a class of mine gets a B." But it was clear that he had learned a lesson. I might add that in the absence of other marks the Bs were of no effect, so no great harm was done. I would be happier if I could be sure that similar anomalies would be caught and properly dealt with today.

(To digress: I recently heard that the University of Toronto has advised faculty to use "in-class grading" as much as possible in view of the current plagiarism of term papers from the Internet as well as from commercial vendors. I was considered eccentric, as usual, when I insisted that all term papers in my evening course must be written in class in a three-hour session. I must have been just a few years ahead of the trend. Even then there was a great deal of commerce in term papers.)

To the list of powerful influences on campus I should add the Faculty Association, which had started at Waterloo College. I do not recall that it challenged the administration very often during the golden years, but in the new era under the province there was a standoff about whether retired faculty might be allowed to continue teaching, and if so, at what financial rates. Two retirees, neither of whom had been able to save enough to support themselves and their spouses properly, or had not been in our pension scheme long enough to earn an adequate retirement income, wanted to go on teaching. Dr. Gerry Noonan, the president of the Faculty Association, led a campaign that resulted in the general policy that faculty might go on teaching, but at reduced stipends. That has meant, too, that the retired faculty of Waterloo Lutheran University and Wilfrid Laurier University tend to be regarded as part of the campus family to an extent that may be unique. By the way, Dr. Noonan won that power struggle, but when, at my retirement, his name was put forward as a possible new chair of English, the president he had worsted in the battle was able to refuse the nomination.

Finally, other officials should be mentioned in other contexts. The Dean of Men and the Dean of Women succeeded the *Hausvater and Hausmutter* of the old days, but the Dean of Women was finally dropped and we then had a Student Dean (a man). I suppose the student counsellors took over, but I regretted the departure of Dean Brandon, an ex-Wren, and a sensible, worldly woman who was a voice for sanity on campus.

We had a chaplain, and in time we had a development officer and a marketing man. The Registrar's Office was taking on its share of power, and the financial area was under the firm control of Dr. Giesbrecht, who was later given an honorary degree. Perhaps the latter was where the real power was.

The head of extension, Professor Clark, exercised a great deal of power, but always with a tactful regard to the rights of everyone, including faculty and students. In spite of his consideration and fairness, he could not avoid getting involved in the final dispute that brought an end to the reign of Dr. Villaume.

CHAPTER III

Heresy Hunts

W HEN SPEAKING OF POWER—especially in the context of a church-related university—the power of belief, whether exerted in the interests of a certain belief or in the hope of spreading it and stamping out other beliefs, must come into our story. When Waterloo College became a Lutheran university, it inherited a rather easygoing approach to beliefs—political or religious. Most employees were Lutheran or vaguely Protestant. In political thought they were mostly Liberal or Conservative with a few exceptions, but I do not recall any disagreements based on party loyalties.

When the synod decided that the college would go its own way, becoming before long a Lutheran university, it was not surprising that questions might be asked about the religious connection. Was it sensible for Lutherans to give financial support to an institution that did not seem to distinguish between correct Lutheran beliefs and those not as clear or as acceptable?

In the time of President Axford (1959-61) I do not recall much energy devoted to defending beliefs. We were too busy recruiting students and faculty, and demonstrating to the community at large that we were alive and deserved to be. President Villaume's reign (1961-67) was a different tale, marked by two crises concerning belief, one to do with articles of faith, and the other the infamous ".Christ or Coffee" confrontation, both of which I will describe shortly.

Who would be interested in working religious differences up into material for headlines? We had a chaplain who I am sure was an authority on Lutheran theology, but he showed little fervour for religious controversy. He was, unusually, of Welsh origin, born in India to Lutheran missionaries, and speaking nothing but Telugu until he went to school. He was highly musical and culturally vague, seeming to feel that here, as in India, there was room for all kinds. If one were interested in purging the university of unbelievers, or wrong believers, he was one of the last persons to be helpful.

Whose responsibility was it? If you wanted to start a holy war to whom would you appeal? The president of the board and the president of the university had the power. Did they have the will? I think the former did, to a degree, though he was open to argument. I am not sure that the university president would have started a crusade on his own, but unfortunately we had acquired a zealot to lecture in the History Department, and, on the side, to stand up for what he deemed to be orthodoxy. He was an American who had been converted to Lutheranism—a particularly conservative branch of it, I believe—and he was eager to defend the faith. He may have had Welsh origins too, or at least Scottish Border ones, his name being John Warwick Montgomery. He was tall, lean, not bad looking and, in his way, perhaps charismatic.

He had written his own version of world history, which he used in his course. Students were required to buy the photocopied volumes, and on his departure the bookstore was left with heaps of his texts, completely useless since no one else would endorse a book that dealt mostly with supposed good guys (Protestants) and bad guys (Roman Catholics or anyone slightly liberal in thought). Professor Montgomery paid for the remainders himself. Unexpectedly, he was perhaps our most popular lecturer. He defied a class to withstand his close arguments and his excited delivery, and he was innovative. For instance, when he became exasperated by the carelessness of his students in the matter of proper manuscript form, he devised a game in which each student became a quotation mark, a footnote, or whatever, and he finally assembled them all on stage in the right order.

I recall one of our students coming from one of his lectures in a state of hilarity. Professor Montgomery had been scolding the popes and she—a good Roman Catholic—was much entertained. She told me that he was one of the best professors she ever had. In fact, his students and colleagues in the History Department remember him fondly. He created an atmosphere of enthusiasm for his subject, and of concern for their academic and personal well-being.

I stayed very much out of his way. First, I suspected that if he ever had the opportunity to talk to me at length he might trap me into giving some sign that I was not unconditionally a believer in Justification by Faith, and that our authorities would hear of it. He may have been suspicious of Anglicans (Episcopalians) in general, thinking I was one.

In fact, one winter when I taught a Saturday morning extension class in Mount Forest, I used to drive up alone in my Volkswagen beetle and stay overnight, rather than ride back on Saturday in comfort with the zealot. Not only did I want to avoid theological argument, but in addition I felt a little uneasy in the presence of a man who worked on several books at a time in his basement, hurrying from one table to another to touch up each manuscript, and who may have had an ink stain like Luther's on one wall, marking the place where the devil had appeared to him. (If he didn't have a stash of typewriters, he probably used a fountain pen since ballpoints were not yet ubiquitous. The ink stain was not totally impossible, but not too likely in our twentieth century.)

You might ask what heresies I was hiding. Nothing serious, I assure you. I feel that belief is a private matter, apart from the sharing in a congregational reciting of the creed, and that it is acceptable to lean one way and then another in interpretation, just as one might agree with at least some of the insights of Marx or Freud.

One of our graduates recalls going to Hamilton with a group of students from Waterloo Lutheran University to hear Dr. Montgomery debate against an Episcopalian bishop, James Pike, who had publicly expressed doubts about the Virgin birth and the doctrine of the Trinity. I gather that our representative disputant was an effective champion for orthodoxy on that occasion, and that on campus he engaged in the good fight against error whenever possible. It is not illogical to believe, as I did, that he harried the presidents of the board and the university into purging the campus of heretics.

I want to mention that John Warwick Montgomery was unexpectedly dismissed by the president at the end of an academic year, and he parted to carry on his war in the United States. We wondered if his "enthusiasm" had become too much for President Villaume, who had little patience with suggestions that he might fill his station otherwise than in the ways he found possible and peaceable. Not too long ago, I came across a report in a religious newspaper regarding a Dr. Montgomery who had just split away into a very fundamentalist group from one that was only a little less rigid. The report mentioned also that his wife had at last decided to split from *him* since he had introduced another lady into his home, and suggested that his wife accept her as part of their marriage. Old Testament readers will recall that such arrangements might be accepted as biblical, but are not usually associated with modern fundamentalism. While he was on our campus, I never heard that he advocated or adopted the domestic arrangements of the Hebrew prophets.

President Villaume was pressured to make the university more worthy of its church connection and to do something about religious dissent on campus. His response was unusual, and on the surface irreproachable, making use of an administrative technique that was democratic, and at the same time binding. We would decide together what we could agree to believe, and there would be no room for deviation after the decision. It would all be done by committees.

First, he appointed a committee to draw up a draft statement of faith. (I hope *all* the papers relating to the whole exercise are in the archives. I am afraid the names of members of the committee and many other relevant facts have disappeared from my memory—and there are not many others who might recall the details.) One of the members was an Anglican, a member of the English Department, a very amiable man who was unlikely to challenge the ideas the president would bring forward, and I think the other appointees were equally amenable to suggestion. The draft from the committee would be brought to a meeting of faculty, which was to break up into small groups, each of which would make a report on belief, based on the original statement. Then the lesser reports would be collated, and a further declaration based on them would be discussed by the faculty as a whole. Finally, a statement would be voted on—and without doubt accepted—and that would be our creed, at least for the time being.

Everyone recognized the technique; it is now very common, but at that time was fairly new, at least in Waterloo. We thought it came out of President Villaume's former career as a sociologist. I find it hard to recall my feelings at the time: perhaps wonder was predominant. How could anyone who knew anything about the history of religious disputes believe that a subject as combustible as theology could be settled with such common sense! I kept wondering what Luther would have said about the draft. I am pretty sure it contained no mention of Justification by Faith.

We assembled uneasily. President Villaume appeared, very sure of himself, ready to superintend the herding of his "sheep" into their separate discussion groups. The meeting was opened, but before the game could begin a voice at the side called out, "I move that we reject this document completely." Someone quickly seconded him, and the president had no alternative but to discuss the motion. He became furious, his face darkened, and he called for recording equipment to be brought in—but there was no discussion. The question was called for, the motion passed, someone must have moved adjournment, and the meeting was over.

As we came out of the room, I was grabbed and piloted into a car where I found myself hurrying with one or two Lutherans towards the home of the president of the board. They had guessed that he knew of the proposed imposition of orthodoxy and would be waiting for word from the meeting. They also suspected there would be others anxious to present their view of events first, thus the haste. When he heard what had happened, the board president was obviously distressed. I'm afraid he had trusted that these modern techniques of problem-solving would have ended his worries about what connection religion should have with running a university.

The man who had stopped the proceedings was Rudy Pinola, a Finnish American from one of the north-central states. He may have been a Communist; at least he was vocal in his condemnation of what he saw as abuses of power. And he was kind and understanding. He had been reared in poverty on a farm. He told me that when he and his brother had been ready to go on to higher education, his father was diagnosed with cancer of the stomach. In those days, proper medical treatment would have cost the family the farm. The father promptly stopped eating any food or drinking water. It didn't take long—just a week or so—before he died, and the farm was saved to support the sons until they could enter the professions they chose. A man from that background would not have much patience with an attempt to trivialize belief. I should add that he didn't make any attempt to have us agree with *his* beliefs.

The other main religious crisis in the golden years related more to the students than to the faculty: the famous Christ or Coffee headline in the *Cord*. A word about the *Cord* here. The name seems to have had something to do with some support from a local company that made twine in the days of harvesting with binders. The pun on chord and the possible reference to "the tie that binds" mentioned in a popular hymn, may also have had something to do with the name. The idea was that the paper would keep us together, but given student human nature and the always present possibility of controversy, the *Cord* was apt to keep us apart—"us" being the editor, his friends, and the administration. The *Cord* advisor was an unfortunate faculty member who was supposed to act as censor, and was blamed whenever the editor annoyed the president. I was advisor for the least time possible and retired gladly, having survived a confrontation in which the editor refused to back down— and was not expelled, perhaps because he came from a pastor's family. I have forgotten the subject of the offending editorial, but I do seem to remember that we heard that in his later travels the editor erected a small tent in Red Square in order to protest against some Soviet abuse of power. He was removed and sent on his way without being put in a gulag. (This must have been in a period of détente.) You can see the kind of student we were likely to have as editor.

The Christ or Coffee headline writer was of that kind. He has since made a career of broadcasting grumblings about the status quo, though he has done nothing as spectacular as challenge the

Soviets—but he *did* challenge President Villaume, and if he had been identified he would have been expelled, and we would have had the newspaper publishing stories about our intolerance.

The headline told of the locking of the Torque Room in chapel time. Our academic day had a vacant slot in the morning for chapel. But not only did we have a nice new chapel, we had a new eating place called the Torque Room, where faculty, staff, and students all ate, drank coffee, played chess, and argued. As you might guess, more students were going to the Torque Room than to chapel, so the president, acting decisively as usual, had the Torque Room locked in chapel time. You can imagine the fuss. Gradually it all died down. The Torque Room reopened, and the writer of this headline was not caught. Graduates from that time have not forgotten the uproar, though one assures me that she is still proud she stood up for Christ against coffee.

CHAPTER IV

Values: Family and Otherwise

F POWER IS EXERTED IN THE NAME OF BELIEF, it is no less found in
dealings with differences of opinion about morality, which may
derive from the Bible, the Koran, or other sacred texts, or may be tra-
ditionally connected with the customs of those societies in which
certain beliefs prevailed. For instance, in early Christian times there
were disputes about veils for women that originated partly from
biblical metaphors regarding veils, and partly from traditional cos-
tume. More serious are differences of opinion regarding the family
and family relations, namely differences outlined in 1997 in a new
papal encyclical condemning all kinds of family planning. Even in
our times, there have been murders in the name of pro-abortion,
and adulterous women have been executed.

Though our seminary students studied moral problems in some
of their courses at Waterloo Lutheran University, I do not recall
that in the golden years we had any open discussion of morality or
any obvious dissension. I do recall some disapproval of a new psychology professor who shocked some people by his use of sexual
terminology in class, not what we might think of as obscenities, but
medical terms, or the like. The objector was a courtly Southern
Baptist from Missouri who might not have protested if men and
women had not been in the same classroom, hearing the explicit language together.

President Villaume seemed to be in favour of family values. The
people of the university would be a family and he would be the

head. He had a president's house built in the midst of residences, the
dining hall, and medical services; we suggested that he hoped to be
able to see into each residence bedroom, but that was of course an
exaggeration.

He set up a regime of family dinners in the dining hall. Faculty
members were required to act as parents, one or two of us at each
table, guiding the conversation and creating an atmosphere of affection and understanding that one might find in a utopia, but which
was somewhat unlike that in most families. I admit that many students liked the innovation, but it made me feel most uncomfortable.
The idea of university students being treated as children at a time
when they should begin making their own lives as adults seemed to
me to be foreign to our traditions. In fact, the president's plan probably came from his American experience with small colleges where
freshmen tended to be at least a year younger than our students
and were perhaps less likely to value their new-found autonomy.

My objections may have come from the fact that I had had more
experience in dining with students than most of my colleagues,
from my time as mistress in a church boarding school to my year as
don at University College, Toronto. Whatever the reason, I was
never happy being *in loco parentis*, and I think most students were
better off dining in casual groupings to which they might invite a
faculty member to chat in a sociable way.

I learned more about the president's views on morality when I
proposed to offer a summer course on eighteenth-century English
drama, in London. One of our faculty members was in England,
working on the subject, and she was enthusiastic about taking students to the actual eighteenth-century theatres or to their former
locations as part of the curriculum. Our president approved the plan
and gave me leave to make arrangements. I got in touch with the
theological school at King's College, London, and was invited to
visit their residence, which would have enough vacancies in summer
to accommodate our students. The location, on the edge of a common, was delightful; the building was quite new and well designed
for its purposes; the woman in charge was charming and sensible. I
had a pleasant tea with her, we agreed on terms, and I paid her a
deposit to retain the places for our students. When I told President

Villaume about the arrangements, he was as pleased as I was. But a day or so later I received a personal telephone call from him. He had been going over the details, and it appeared then that men and women would be living under the same roof. Could that be true? I had to confess that it was. Oh, then, the whole scheme was impossible. By that time it was too late to find other accommodation, and I knew it would have been just about impossible to find anything as well suited to our needs, so I had to cancel—and I lost my deposit. I was also very annoyed by the evident concern for appearance, as well as for the rigorous separation of the sexes: an expression of power in controlling the lives of others in the name of morality.

Anyone who recalls the Villaume era, or who has heard campus legends about his time, will be wondering how I could have written thus far on the moral flavour of his reign without betraying some sense of irony, because the general impression was that he, himself, had not avoided offence against propriety, or had at least covered up suggestions of scandal. To deal further with the subject, it might be well to stop and describe Dr. William J. Villaume.

He came from Louisiana; his name was probably Creole in origin. We knew little about him, but rumour had given tantalizing bits of what may have been misinformation. We heard he had been a convert to Lutheranism. We knew he was ordained and that his academic specialty was social work. It was said that he had played some part in the labour troubles on the New York docks; I always had visions of Marlon Brando in *On the Waterfront* when that episode was mentioned. William Villaume had later become what our Southern Baptist colleague despised: a Madison Avenue religionist. Our friend said that they had spent their lives greeting one another while getting on and off planes, carrying handsome briefcases. Our former president's most recent achievement had been forcing the Unitarians out of the World Council of Churches—or so we were told.

He was not aware that Canada was not the United States. If we protested some of his suggestions—"You don't do that in Canada"—he replied, "Well, you should." Even now, I believe he is remembered at Queen's Park as having bombarded the ministers with accusations about their unfairness in withholding grants from us, not realizing that in Canada one really influences governments in much more indirect ways. In arguments with him it was possible to make a point by finding some American analogy. For instance, when Dr. Overgaard suggested that the Honourable W. Ross Macdonald, former Speaker of our House of Commons, would be a good choice as our chancellor, the president would hear nothing of it until he was asked, "Do you know of Sam Rayburn [Speaker of the US House]?" "Oh, yes, he's a great friend of mine," he replied. "Well, Ross Macdonald is the Sam Rayburn of Canada," he was told. That ended the objections, and we gained a kindly and influential chancellor.

Our president would have made his mark by changing the whole aspect of university-government relations in Ontario if one of his schemes had worked out. Queen's Park seemed to be opposed to church-related institutions, but President Villaume deduced from American examples that there might be a political force in the voters from the fundamentalist camp, so he made overtures to groups pretty far to the right in religion—and otherwise—to see if he could form some kind of alliance. Some of these groups had schools or colleges, and others would no doubt have been delighted to have postsecondary institutions in which they could control the ideology and the moral climate, but there was no chance that the Ontario government would give them charters. We had a charter and could have taken them on as affiliates, though I cannot imagine how we could have become responsible for their academic standards. True, we had a Mennonite affiliate, but the Mennonites had inquired into *our* academic standing before joining us and were determined to keep theirs as high as possible. After all, being situated in Winnipeg, they were in some competition with the University of Manitoba.

The overtures to minority religious groups were not well received on our campus. Many of us took fright because we envisioned our turning into a Canadian Bob Jones University, which may have been all very well in South Carolina, but had implications of divisiveness and political strife that we did not wish to see in Ontario, as well as being a threat to academic freedom. Memories of the McCarthy era were still warning us against mixing politics and academia any more than necessary. Our president must have been finally convinced that it could not come to fruition. From his point of view, if it had succeeded, it would have been a victory over the people in Queen's Park who would not respond to his arguments, and it would have shown who really had power—himself. I never had any impression that he shared the religious views of the groups with which he wanted to be affiliated, but I don't think that mattered as long as he could create a party.

But let us give him his due. He provided much of the impetus that transformed a tiny institution to a university with about six thousand students, partly through his program of erecting more buildings on the original campus. At one time, there was a move to sell some of the land within the area bounded by four streets, but that was defeated. Still, by the end of his regime, passersby could see that there was action around the university, though not everyone quite understood what was going on. At the same time, he was creating the administrative structure that would grow into Wilfrid Laurier University. There was so much to be done. I recall, for instance, the choosing of designs and colours for academic regalia, the drawing up of rituals for convocation, and the moving of ecclesiastical processions down University Avenue to bless new buildings, just small parts of the drive towards our acceptance in the academic community. We had always had the respect of our colleagues on other campuses for our courses, and for the achievements of our graduates, but a university needs more than that to feel secure.

Much as we now try to depersonalize our leaders in the name of political correctness, it is still hard to ignore the human being when summing up achievements, and as a man our president had, almost from the beginning, created impressions that kept us in some doubt about his real values and intentions. It appeared, for example, that there were anomalies in his domestic situation that were later rectified by divorce and remarriage.

How did the evident moral anomalies affect our university? I don't think it encouraged faculty, staff, or students to overstep the bounds of what was acceptable behaviour in any obvious way. The loosening of rules that came in the late 1960s—but for us more in the early 1970s—was part of the cultural change that swept over

North America and Europe then, and had as much to do with student visits to Amsterdam as with what happened on one campus.

What finally ended Dr. Villaume's presidency was not his private life but a dispute about the appointment of the head of our popular summer school in Orillia. From the beginning of his tenure, our president had apparently identified Dr. Fred Little as a possible rival. The Little family had a long history of leadership on our campus. Dr. C.H. Little had been president of Waterloo College School from 1918 to 1920. His two sons, Arthur and Fred, were on our faculty. Fred had been an especially brilliant student. I believe he had only one mark that was less than an A in his undergraduate career, and he went on to do a doctorate at one of the top American universities. At one of the first meetings of some of our faculty with Dr. Villaume, I had supported Fred in a relatively unimportant challenge regarding a decision of the president (which I think was the origin of his distrust of me and later prompted him to a couple of weak efforts to dislodge me).

Fred had served very well in building up the extension work in Orillia that contributed so much to our financial well-being. In 1967 he was apparently being considered for the presidency of Canmore College, but could not make a final decision about going to Orillia in time to suit Dr. Villaume, who deviously went ahead and appointed George Tompkins, a very junior member of our faculty, to head the session there. From that time on, the waters become more and more muddy. Dr. Little even accused President Villaume of blackmail in demanding he reply by a certain date or forfeit his acting chairmanship. Consequently, Dr. Little gladly surrendered the position for the sake of retaining his integrity, refusing to be intimidated by President Villaume. In the appendix are copies of some letters relating to the incident. A future historian of academic politics may find them interesting.

The department heads had become more and more dubious about President Villaume's leadership. You could not even say he led. He made his decisions, acted on them, and then announced them. His most trusted advisor, the head of the seminary, was appealed to, but he pointed out that the president was a "loner" who listened to no advice. Finally, partly in support of Fred Little, department heads voted in a secret ballot to protest to the board of governors. This led to the appointment of a consulting firm to examine our earlier administrative practices, and that caused President Villaume to resign. Given his personality, one could have expected nothing less. He returned in due time to the United States and resumed his place in the Lutheran world.

To sum up the contributions of Dr. William J. Villaume to Waterloo Lutheran University, I turn to two documents from the university's archives. The first, an obituary, reveals that President Villaume, in spite of the Louisiana connection, was born in Brooklyn, and abandoned as a child. One would like to know the intervening history, but it is clear that from that inauspicious beginning he rose to participate in the higher councils of the United States and Canada.

WILLIAM VILLAUME, LUTHERAN PASTOR, 80

The Rev. Dr. William J. Villaume, a Lutheran minister who pursued prominent parallel careers as pastor, educator and national religious administrator, died on Monday at his home in Corpus Christi, Tex. He was 80.

The cause was emphysema, his family said.

In a life that took him from a troubled childhood in Brooklyn to the highest councils of Protestantism in the United States, Dr. Villaume was a pastor of three churches, served as president of three major colleges and headed two major departments of the National Council of Churches in New York. In the 1950's, President Dwight D. Eisenhower asked him to deliver an inaugural prayer and made him a Federal adviser on child welfare, the elderly, housing and education.

Dr. Villaume was born in Brooklyn and abandoned as a child. He graduated from Wagner College on Staten Island, began his ministry at St. Peter's in Manhattan and later served as pastor of churches in Middletown, N.Y., Fitchburg, Mass., and Rindge, N.H.

He is survived by his wife, Arlette; two sons, William, of Auburn, Ala., and James, of Corpus Christi; two daughters, Jean Elizabeth Aldridge of Leawood, Kan., and Nancy Lynne Tieeszen of Sioux Falls, S.D.; nine grandchildren, and two brothers, Louis of Lake Charles, La., and Jacques, of Baton Rouge.

His achievements are summarized in the second item, an article from the *Laurier News*, April 11, 1995, which reads as follows:

PASTORATE FIRST LOVE OF WLU PRESIDENT

Dr. William John Villaume, who served as the first president of Waterloo Lutheran University from 1961 through 1967, died in Corpus Christi, Texas, late last month.

Villaume came to the University from a position with the Department of Social Welfare of the National Council of the Churches of Christ in the United States.

Ordained in 1938, Villaume held a Master of Science degree in Social Work and a PhD in Sociology and Social Ethics.

He had been a visiting lecturer at the graduate school for advanced studies in social welfare at Brandeis University, and was co-chair of the planning committee on religion for the 1961 White House conference on aging. He served as a consultant to the US government on several occasions in the areas of child welfare, aging, housing, education, and public assistance.

"Especially memorable," he said in a career summary sent to University Relations in the 1980s, "were experiences as vice-chairman and program chairman of the Golden Anniversary White House Conference on Children and Youth (when I spoke preceding President Eisenhower at the Opening Plenary Session in the University of Maryland field house); as the preacher at the Baccalaureate Service at the famed Tuskegee Institute in Alabama on the day when the Commencement address was delivered by Martin Luther King, Jr.; as one of three persons who prepared the final report of the national Advisory Council on Public Assistance (by Act of Congress, 1958); as a delegate to the World Conference on Faith and Order of the World Council of Churches and the Council's Conference on the Role of the Churches in International Migration."

On leaving WLU, Villaume became President of Pierce College in Athens, Greece, then returned to a pastorate, described as his "first love," in Fitchburg, Massachusetts. He retired in 1979, and in 1983 organized a new church in Rindge, New Hampshire. He was presented with an honorary doctorate from WLU in 1986.

Villaume moved into the presidency at the beginning of a decade of growth and change for the institution—the first section of Clara Conrad Hall opened in 1961, the Dining Hall, Student's Union Building, Theatre Auditorium, and West Hall, a men's residence, were all completed and dedicated in 1962. In 1963, the Seminary building was finished and dedicated, as were the east wing of the Arts Building, East Hall (another men's residence), and the first addition to Clara Conrad. Two years later, the first two floors of the Library were constructed.

In a newspaper interview in 1963, and at the beginning of a $15 million expansion, Villaume drew the line on growth. The University was proud of its 72 courses that had registrations of under 10 students, and of its small, compact, one-block campus, he told the interviewer. Once the then-enrolment of 1,300 reached 1,800, he said, "enrolment will be curbed and WLU will remain a relatively small university."

"We are concerned here with the development of the total person; intellectually first, but also the social and religious aspects.

"We are trying to make a university education mean something more than just academics; we are trying to develop what Toynbee calls the leaders for a creative minority.... And I know of no way to doing this when you have thousands and thousands of students. It can't be done on a production-line basis."

Villaume's widow, Arlette, is expected to visit the area in May, at which time a memorial service for the late president will be arranged by the President's Office.

CHAPTER V

Marketing

IN THE ACADEMIC STRUGGLE FOR SURVIVAL in the Ontario of the early sixties, the powerful universities that might be expected to survive, barring unlikely catastrophe, were Toronto and Queen's. Western and McMaster were moving into similarly impregnable positions, with perhaps a little more unease shown in manoeuvres to strengthen programs and attract benefactors. The new universities, once they had met local needs, would have to develop further attractions if they were to be successful rivals in the new academic arena. Institutions clustered in the southwestern parts of the province, looking to the same market for students and donors, would have to become as competitive as if they were similar commercial organizations, vying for the same clients.

Waterloo Lutheran University, in the same city as the University of Waterloo, was particularly vulnerable, and became especially competitive—though I am not sure that the larger rival was ever aware that there was any contest. The co-op engineering program which had been the excuse for founding a new post-secondary institution, through its wide publicity and the approval of industry, had put the University of Waterloo on the way to competing on the same level as the older universities. What could a tiny, church-related body show to catch and hold public attention?

We had to market ourselves, though we never put it as crudely as that—and we had several advantages. For a short time we could move ahead of the University of Waterloo in innovation because it had to get organized first to work out relationships and responsibilities. We could carry on as we had since 1911, yet shift course for new and more interesting ventures without fuss. We had plenty of imagination and energy on our own, but I must concede that without professional help we would not have succeeded so well and so soon.

I shall mention later the conferring of a doctorate on Urho Kaleve Kekkonen, president of Finland. Our administrators, in choosing candidates for honorary degrees, were drawing attention to Lutherans who were world renowned, and from origins other than the German background of most of the local members of a minority church group. The public was reminded that Lutheranism was the religion of the majority in Scandinavia, and not just of some citizens of Waterloo County.

Behind most of our first achievements in getting public recognition was another northern Lutheran, this time a Dane, Dick Hermanson, a public relations professional. We had heard that his PR achievements included the addition of bananas to the other ornaments on Carmen Miranda's hats, and the removal of a certain brand of groceries from the shelves of a supermarket chain in Quebec. The bananas figured in photographs that the press seized upon, thus giving the Brazilian icon immediate fame as an entertainer. About the supermarket story I know nothing more—but the mind behind both achievements was creative, offbeat, and relentless, and the personality was one that was comfortable and popular anywhere, especially in gatherings of the press. In other words, his specialty was not only unusual ideas but manipulation as well. He soon knew everyone in Kitchener and Waterloo who had anything to do with publicity and, I suspect, knew how each could be pressured, bullied, or tempted into giving us some attention. For instance, he persuaded the *K–W Record* to give prominent billing to an award I had won after they had buried it in another story. I asked if he had played poker for the victory, but he just laughed. At the reporters' club, or elsewhere, he had learned something he could trade for that favour: an embarrassing item about a junior editor to be suppressed in exchange for a local news scoop that would keep

Waterloo Lutheran University before the public. We never knew his methods, but we benefited from his success.

He may have had another reason than ordinary professionalism for his hard work for us. As a Scandinavian Lutheran, he probably enjoyed showing the public that his church and its Canadian university were not only for the children of German-Canadian farmers in the hinterland, worthy as they might be, but part of a tradition of culture and learning pre-dating co-op engineering and other modern innovations. However, he may have shown too much interest in Waterloo Lutheran University and its aims. For some reason, having to do, I was told, with a power struggle between the president and director of publicity, he was in time forced to resign and a much more malleable individual took his place. He went knowing that there was no room on the campus for two strong individuals. As a professional, he knew when to concede defeat. He remained in the area, I believe, active in his church and, it was said, in the community. I do not know who holds the official title of founder of Oktoberfest, which is now regarded as a local tradition, but I did hear that the idea had been Hermanson's.

While he was with Waterloo Lutheran University, his two most obvious contributions were our entry into the bed-pushing contest and our winter festival. Both seem now as far away as the Crusades. Political correctness and fashion may have made them outmoded, like much that used to be typical of college life. I digress to mention that not too long ago an unwise don, perhaps wishing to relieve winter boredom, suggested to some male students that they might stage an old-fashioned panty raid, which they did. And the university got publicity.

Back in the early 1960s, bed pushing was fun. Junior faculty became enthusiastic supporters, providing rest and refreshments for the participants at each stage, everyone encouraged by the lights and cameras and the bonhomie. Oddly enough, by today's standards, I don't think our students pushed a hospital bed from London to Waterloo overnight to support any good cause or to protest against some injustice; they were merely trying to beat the records set by other universities. Students, faculty, and faculty wives were requisitioned, some to provide coffee at a rest stop in the middle of the night, some to push, and the rest to provide the complex infrastructure needed for an enterprise of this kind. The papers could not ignore this event, and again we were favourably in the public eye.

There is a legend that the president of our neighbouring university kidnapped the bed for a time, but was persuaded to release it when Dick Hermanson went to him and threatened to tell all to the newspapers. In any event, it did get to Ottawa somehow, where the chief of police refused to allow it to be pushed along the streets. A group of MPs, probably inspired by our local representative, hosted a reception for the bed pushers on Parliament Hill. More publicity, coast to coast. The visit of the "Bonhomme Carnivale" to Waterloo for a weekend was an exchange for this visit of Waterloo Lutheran University to Ottawa. I don't recall much about the arrival of the "Bonhomme Carnival," except that it was an example of a friendly connection with our neighbours to the east.

Another idea was that during the winter festival the campus would be adorned with ice sculptures, but almost always our festival was coincidental with a January thaw. I recall an ice effigy of Dr. Overgaard, director of the School of Business, wearing red Hush Puppies. Since the local manufacturer of Hush Puppies was president of our board, and Herman really did wear a red pair as a joke, no one could miss the two-sided humour.

The winter festivals that involved the crowning of a campus queen came to an end in the 1970s, with demonstrations of protest from local feminists against the stereotyping of campus females as ornaments, especially coming from "the other university." I have just been looking at some photographs of the crowning of the queen, and must agree that she and her attendants tended to be pretty, even beautiful, carefully coiffed and made up. (The Avon lady made regular visits to the girls' residences, I was told.) In the early photographs their bouffant gowns revealed what I'm sure was carefully powdered flesh. Later, the young women changed with fashion and looked less like Doris Day. The 1960s counter-culture breaking of the mould would seem to have banished all that forever, except that a stray issue of a women's magazine I glanced at when visiting my hairdresser recently featured an article on how to make oneself beautiful with cosmetics in lieu of surgery. But back in the 1960s, good looks were expected of a woman—natural if possible, enhanced by art, or created by illusion, if not.

When Dick Hermanson disappeared from campus, we were again lucky when a young Englishman called Barry Lyon was hired in his place. He was just as imaginative as Dick Hermanson, with a quirky sense of humour, and was perhaps more of a team player, involving his colleagues on campus in his schemes. The one that comes first to my mind involves a yellow 1930 Ruxton Roadster, owned by the Craven A Foundation of Toronto (and well before the No Smoking revolution). It was equipped with licence plates, reading WLU4ME and WLU4U and was to be driven by our president of the time, Frank Peters, a professor of psychology and a Mennonite minister. Photographs of president and vehicle were accompanied by a slogan, A Touch of Class. I have asked Barry where he got the phrase. He says it just came to him. People read their own meaning into the words, but I think in general it conveyed the message that Waterloo Lutheran University was a bit ahead of the times.

The president's sense of humour complemented that of his PR man, so he was merely amused when Barry and friends managed to remove his car from his usual parking lot and substitute a Mennonite buggy, complete with horse. That photograph in the press didn't do us any harm either.

I cannot find out if the following story is apocryphal or not, but Barry assures me it is worth repeating. I once heard that our president, Dr. Peters, was on the Guelph highway at night, enjoying a drive in his vintage car, when he was stopped by the highway patrol and informed him that he had been exceeding the speed limit. Since he hadn't seen any pursuing vehicle, he asked how his speed could have been known. The officer merely waved his hand to the heavens—I gather that a helicopter had been on duty up there. Dr. Peters raised the Bible that he had on the seat beside him and said, "Oh, if that is where your information comes from, I'll confess, I *was* a bit over the limit." After a hearty laugh, the policeman said, "Well, next time be more careful, Reverend," and the conversation was over. For public relations: Waterloo Lutheran University was thus shown to be associated with a denomination other than Lutheran,

WLU could take a joke about its religious affiliation, and WLU's president shared with ordinary mortals an affinity for speed. I was once reminded that Dr. Peters also had a motorbike. I don't recall seeing him suitably dressed for mounting *that* vehicle, but I can imagine the spectacle. Again he was presenting something other than an image of dull religiosity.

When the university's change of status necessitated a change of name, Barry Lyon designed a calendar cover of reflecting glass on which you read at one angle the old name, and at another angle the new, with the initials remaining the same as you moved the glass. The calendars were given to high schools where such gimmicks were sure to catch attention, as were replicas of the licence plates on the Ruxton Roadster, thus giving youthful minds an impression of Waterloo Lutheran University as a place that was "cool."

One more example: to publicize the name change, our PR people bought a full-page ad in *Time*, showing a WLU sweatshirt on a coat hanger with the initials painted out, and then with the initials painted in. Barry tells me it was "cute," which is perhaps the word for all his ideas, as in endearing with their innocuous wit, and also "acute," because of their underlying significance.

When the romantic winter festival ended in a more enlightened age, it was replaced by a week of worthy effort in honour of something. Didn't we once have an Arthurian festival at the end of which the chief organizer really did depart for Avalon, much lamented? That was one of the sad memories of those times. By 1997 there was still some sort of marking of January festival time, but it appears to be more a matter of silly races in the halls than of general artistic or physical exertion. The days when students wrote the script and songs, acted, sang, and danced in college shows such as the old Purple and Gold Revues are long gone.

Until his departure, Dick Hermanson was involved in all our relations with the public, but he did not need to initiate all our attention-getting activities. Some had become campus customs, such as the choir tours. Others were generated by groups or individuals. Waterloo College had a strong drama tradition, and it continued at Waterloo Lutheran University. Before the "split," I had arranged for our institution to sponsor an appearance of the Stratford

Theatre Company in Waterloo, and I saw no reason to cancel it because we were now on our own. However, performers of *The Merchant of Venice* gave a persuasive reading that was too realistic for some of the spectators. The morning after the performance, I received an indignant telephone call from a faculty wife at the new University of Waterloo, upbraiding me for what she considered the anti-Semitism of the production. "Shylock was just like the man at the corner store," she said, which was not surprising since a number of the best Canadian actors in the company were Jewish. I didn't feel that the fact that Shylock seemed a sympathetic character and yet was the villain was my fault (after all, Shakespeare had something to do with it), and I told her to direct her complaints to the producer.

That was our first and last sponsorship of an outside production, I believe, but our own theatre flourished under committees staffed by alumni and community friends, as well as by faculty and staff. There was at least one major production on campus each year, the director being a temporary import—sometimes from afar. I seem to remember that one of them was an Afghan. The only play I recall in any detail was *The Fantasticks*, which I think was produced entirely by students.

For a time we had a yearly festival of plays from other cultures: French, Russian, German. An excerpt from *Mother Courage* remains with me (those were the Brecht years), and a French play—was it *Ici On Parle Anglais*? The producer of the latter was an *assistante* from France, Mme Perrier, who had studied at the Comédie-Française in her youth, but had been prevented from acting by her relatives who felt that it was beneath them to have an actress in the family.

The central figure of theatre on campus was a professor of English, James Clark, who taught the general course on the history of drama—meaning a study of significant plays. His enthusiasm was caught by many of his students, some of whom later made their living in the theatre. One became wardrobe mistress at Stratford; one has been part of the Toronto drama scene for years. I believe Professor Clark's favourite dramatist was Shaw: generations of our graduates dared to make changes in their lives because Shaw and the professor had taught them to see through shams. Before the era of political correctness could arise, the eras of conformity and suppression had to end, and while laughing at a Shavian character, in particular, the audience might go on to laugh at convention and hierarchy in general.

Professor Clark was one of the two members of our English Department who died in harness. A graduate who telephoned me from Chicago, where she was a professor of English, could only say, "We loved him."

Dr. Lorna Berman, who had been a faculty member of the French section of the Romance Languages Department and later the chair, gave me a copy of a program for a soirée on February 7, 1963, directed by Mme Perrier, which she had found when going through her files. I append the program as it was, asking the reader to note especially the list of patrons that reminds us of a piece of history not often recalled today. After the Second World War, the new France, unbowed yet sensitive about its reputation among those who, while praising de Gaulle, the liberator, had not forgotten Pétain, the Third Reich collaborator, set out to re-educate the world about French achievements, and especially about French language and culture. (Was Malraux the head of the enterprise?) Thus we had on-campus, for an evening of French music and drama, the French consul général and the vice consul, and we had Mme Odile Martz-Perrier.

In view of the discovery of the program, perhaps I should say something more about her. She was, I believe, a widow, and I seem to recall that the first half of her hyphenated name referred to her first husband, who possibly manufactured pianos. The second husband seems to have been equally successful, but was by then also dead. I'm not sure if Madame would have approved of divorce, since she had a leaning towards orthodoxy. She once told me that as a concession to tradition her devoutly atheist father always cut a cross on the top of the family loaf of bread before he carved the first slice. Divorced or widowed, she was alone at a certain age, and some sort of dependant of the French government. She told stories of being attached to an embassy in Spanish America, with details of the infighting that took place there—and which I gathered was just a tradition of French officialdom.

On our pacific campus she didn't find a similar tradition, but she endeavoured to create one. For starters, she hated anyone who spoke French with a Spanish accent and was heard to scream at one such in the corridor—the poor man was a colleague in romance languages who had dared to compliment her in his Spanish-accented French; to make it worse, he was Catalan. I gather that she made many enemies at Waterloo Lutheran University in the name of French culture and language.

She put up with me for a long time because I carefully avoided saying anything in French within her hearing. She understood quite a lot of English, so I could listen to her remarks in her language and reply in my own. I fell into disfavour after writing her a letter in English, thanking her for something or other, and using the forms approved by most polite Canadians. I received a blazing reply, castigating me for my want of respect. I knew perfectly well what the French forms were, but they would have sounded false in an English epistle; Madame Martz-Perrier was not going to allow me that excuse. Since by that time she had left the campus, I didn't bother to follow up, and I lost touch without any regret.

Fortunately we had students then who could appreciate her as a museum piece. One of them told me that at an evening party she had given for students in her Toronto apartment, she had inveigled him out on the balcony with her, and he added, "For the first time I realized what my mother had always warned me against." That he could react with amusement suggested to me that our students were ready to survive in the wicked, multicultural world that awaited them.

And it did them no harm to hear the French of the Comédie-Française of Paris, France.

WATERLOO UNIVERSITY COLLEGE

French Artistic Evening (*Soirée*)

Waterloo Lutheran University
Theatre Auditorium

February 7, 1963, 8:00 P.M.

Under the patronage of
Mr. Guy Scalabre, *Consul Général de France à Toronto*
Mr. Daniel Bornstein, *Vice-Consul*
Dr. W.J. Villaume, *President of WLU*
Dr. L.H. Schaus, *Dean of WUC*
Dr. N.H. Tayler, *Chairman of Romance Languages*
with the co-operation of students of the French Course
Madame Odile Perrier, *Producer*

PART ONE

French and Canadian Songs
Music ... Songs ... Dancing—Fantaisies musicales—Mr. D. Borny
1. *Suzannah*
2. *Reviens Valse moderne*

Theatrical Part
Le Malade Imaginaire—ACT I: scenes 4 and 5—Molière

Personnages
Argan, Mr. M. Bernardo
Angélique, Miss J. Machesney
Toinette, Miss S. Harre

INTERMISSION

PART TWO

French and Canadian Songs
Music ... Songs ... Dancing—Fantaisies musicales—Mr. D. Borny
1. *Vodka! Vodka!*
2. *Ming-Tchoung-Li-Wang et Lao-Tse*
By the Choir of WUC under the direction of Mr. C.S. McClain

Theatrical Part
L'anglais tel qu'on le parle—Tristan Bernard
Vaudeville en un acte ... from the repertoire of the
Comédie Française de Paris France

100.001^{ème} Représentation

Please purchase tickets in advance
from
Office of WLU Alliance Française

CHAPTER VI

The Campus Family
and Guests

"WE WERE A FAMILY," said Rich Newbrough, the retiring director of Athletics and Recreation, when we were chatting about the early, uncertain days of Waterloo Lutheran University. "It's as if there was a wall between us," said the retired payroll secretary of her relationship with the faculty at a rather later time. Somewhere between these two impressions lies the real story of the spirit on campus from 1960 to 1973, but in order to get at it one would probably have to examine the background of each individual concerned. In lieu of that, a discussion of various groups may reveal attitudes that affected the emotional climate in the university and either enhanced or detracted from the cohesion necessary for our success as an institution. At the end we will probably find that Rich's remark was appropriate if one remembers that a family is bound by affection, enmity, jealousy, pride, and various other emotional responses.

Rich Newbrough, "Tuffy" Knight, and Fred Nichols represented one group who affected the quality of life on our campus, and later, through Tuffy, the life on the campus of the University of Waterloo, where he became football coach. The three had come from West Virginia—an unlikely provenance for staff of a Canadian Lutheran university. (How did they get there? Were they recruited through our American Lutheran connections?) They even came from the same place; I believe that at least Rich and Tuffy had gone to the same school. They brought an air of assurance and an ease in mingling with others that seems typical of a certain segment of society from the American south. Their easygoing manner had an undertone of courtesy, but there was nothing obsequious about it. They were also literate. I had occasion to receive letters from Tuffy and Rich in answer to my own recognition of their respective retirements from our campus, and in each case it was obvious that their school had taught them to read and write well. In the early days of their guidance of our athletes, I appreciated the fact that football players who took compulsory English courses tried to show interest and respect, however little aptitude they had for the study of literature. Aside, I might remark that another of our American sports imports, who unfortunately didn't stay, persuaded me to let his wife into the Honours English program and made it his business to see that she had time from her domestic responsibilities to read and study. I may have been wrong, but I rather suspected that that tall handsome athlete from the West had at least a little aboriginal blood in his veins—another element in the mix that was our campus family. Not everyone knew, by the way, that a number of our students were from the indigenous peoples, for instance, several members of a gifted (possibly Mohawk) family, and one student from the Parry Sound area who discovered that there were common elements in the story of *Beowulf* and his own ancestral folk tales that probably inspired Longfellow's *Hiawatha*.

To return to the sociable group from West Virginia, their example could not help but influence colleagues and students, giving our university the reputation of being a friendly place. Then how could the woman from payroll have quite the opposite memories? Reminiscing about my life during regular summers in Britain brought back memories I had forgotten—one of them was the realities of the English class system that imposed patterns of behaviour that were second nature to natives. (In general I continued to greet everyone in England much as I would have in Canada, but I kept the rules of etiquette in mind just the same.) One dictum was that on any encounter, if the person of the higher class did not speak first, the other was supposed to remain silent. That involved very complicated comparisons that would have to be made and acted on instantly because the levels of the hierarchy seemed infinite; for instance, an owner of a shop was superior to anyone employed as an assistant, but there would be various gradations of shops. My inform- ant from payroll was expecting the male faculty members, her supe- riors, to speak first when she met them, while they were probably following an old-fashioned Canadian belief that a woman was always the one who should decide first to acknowledge the acquaintance. Because of her aloofness, the men were probably thinking, "Well, she doesn't want to carry our acquaintance outside of her office," while she was thinking that they didn't like her and that there was a wall between them. The protocol of greetings is a tradition of British royalty: the Queen must speak before she can be addressed. On an early visit by Queen Elizabeth to Canada, one VIP in Saskatchewan became the butt of jokes in the eastern press because he asked her, speaking first, "How are the kids?" At least that is the story.

Other cultures were represented on campus too, but in small numbers. I have never hoped to understand the fine points of Ger- man manners, but it seems that our students from Austria or Ger- many just gave up and tried to be like the rest of us, though it may not have been easy. The widow of one of our German professors told me that after his death she found in his desk a paper on which he had written, "I shall never understand this country." Attitudes and forms brought from the University of Heidelberg and from the German army were not like those of Waterloo County. But from another point of view, the integrated members could take on too many Canadian traits. I recall that the wife of a German friend of the University told me that after many years in Canada she and her husband visited their homeland. At a family dinner with her hus- band's brother, the visitors were horrified when the host stopped the meal and addressed them, saying, "We eat correctly in this house!" They never had any idea what they had done to break the rules and were happy to be back in Canada where life was less trying.

All this seems idiotic to me now, but it was important at the time and suggests that, in order to succeed, administrators and per- sonnel of any group need to be sensitive to cultural differences, even if it is not possible to satisfy all codes of conduct.

When I think of individuals in our "family," including those employed in non-academic positions, I do not recall feeling barriers between us. A great many employees were newcomers or the children of newcomers, who were here because they intended to rise in status themselves or through their children. I recall one dining-room lady whose son became a medical doctor; I'm sure she regarded herself as my equal. Many of the children of employees were our students. One student in the English Department, who later taught in a community college, was the daughter of the couple who cooked for the old "Boarding Club" of Waterloo College.

I recall a relationship that was almost affectionate with employees like Ernie, a Swiss groundsman, who told me how much he enjoyed an errand to our office, and "a nice smile." He knew he was in uncertain health and had discussed plans for his family's future with, I believe, Professor Clark. When he collapsed and died in the library, the students, staff, and faculty grieved deeply, demonstrated by the memorial service held in the chapel and presided over by the head of the seminary.

I can visualize some of the "workers" and can recall friendly exchanges of greetings. Several were ex-soldiers, such as one who retained his British accent and told me of his time in Rimini as the Allies advanced north. I was aware that these sweepers and dusters felt that they were as much a part of the university as I was and that their view of its mission and its effectiveness had validity, just as mine had.

The dining hall as it was in the golden years brought us all together, and its employees were especially close to many of us. In its first year or so, we lost Mary, the waitress who had been like an elder sister, providing food for the rest of the family. When she survived one of the early open-heart operations for only a week or two, there was sorrow on campus, and her picture was framed and hung in what is now the Paul Martin Centre (named after Paul Martin, Sr.). To this day I still feel that the staff in the dining hall look on the rest of us as "family," though pre-prepared and frozen food has long replaced the triumphs of some of the best cooks in the Twin Cities. Do I recall that the pastry chef was said to be *the* best? You see, those first cooks were recruited to some extent through Lutheran congregations where everyone would know if Katherine, or Frieda, or Anna could make good pies.

Once a year the dining hall staff could show off at the dinner that brought together the faculty and the board. The masterpiece was always a huge fish surrounded by all the good food from Waterloo County necessary for a feast. I'm not sure it was all good for our arteries, but the meal did wonders for the feeling of fellowship.

An exotic note was added by Dr. Evelyn Boyd, an American member of the English Department, who began the custom of the annual Boar's Head Dinner. Recently, at one of those dinners, I was sad to see that any reference to the original—at Oxford or in Waterloo—was perfunctory. Gone was the carol singing, gone were the mummers and dancers. A few uninterested students traipsed dutifully around the hall, carrying something on a platter, while the audience was largely lined up at the cash bar. Dr. Boyd would not have been amused. I recall that she gave me a quota of linen napkins that I was to hem for the original feast. When I tactfully pointed out that the student committee was perfectly able to sew a hem, she reported that she couldn't trust their work; I suppose that that was a compliment, but in those days I felt I had more to do than sew hems.

That same Dr. Boyd was for a time a strong influence at Waterloo Lutheran University, and later at the University of Waterloo. Surrounded by cigarette smoke and her three untidy dogs, one of which dated from her days working in a hospital for soldiers, she maintained an outpost of Iowa culture. I think Chaucer was her special subject, but she also taught creative writing in which students turned out stories that reminded me of the works of numerous American women who wrote before the Second World War. Such stories would be more impressive now, in the days of women's studies, than they were when students were interested in imitating Faulkner or Joyce—or Frost. She was a retiree from Iowa when she came to us, and when she retired from Waterloo Lutheran University she joined the University of Waterloo and became part of their traditions. An interesting mixture of *A Girl of the Limberlost* and

Flannery O'Connor. She told me that at the time of one family be-
reavement she spent a whole night making strawberry jam, something a character would do in the literature of late medieval England.
They do not make them like her anymore.

CHAPTER VII

Honoured Guests

———— ⚜ ————

As I chronicle my recollections of events and innovations on campus that kept the university's name before the public and, we hoped, drew in students, I should make it clear that though our efforts could still be defined as "marketing" to attract friends and students, we were aware that they improved our own academic lives in many directions. Graduates and professors who recall fondly the early years of Waterloo Lutheran University are to a degree influenced by memories of the interesting people we invited on campus and the diverse activities going on there.

Details of the selection of chancellors and the recipients of honorary doctorates who were among our distinguished visitors will be available to future researchers in the archives of the administration, but I'll mention what seemed particularly interesting to me. Of the chancellors, I recall particularly Euler, Macdonald, and Aird. The choice of William D. Euler established our connection with the Lutheran tradition in Kitchener (Berlin) and Waterloo. He had success in business and in public life along with firm ties to the church. I have only a tantalizing memory of a local disagreement during which an opponent held Euler out of a window of the old Kitchener city hall, threatening to dash him to the pavement. Passions ran strong in local politics then.

I recently heard a story that explains that threat to Senator Euler. Retired English professor Jane Campbell told me that her husband,

Craig Campbell, passed down a family tale about the incident. His father recalled that as a small boy he and his mother happened to be in the vicinity of the old city hall and he saw his father pulling a man from a window. It seems that the Kitchener city council had passed a rule that all councillors must take the oath of allegiance and kiss the flag. Mr. Euler refused to do either, whereupon someone grabbed him and threatened to throw him out the window if he did not comply. Mr. Campbell, while disapproving of Mr. Euler's stand, was not in favour of murder and came to his rescue, hauling the future senator to safety. But he and his family did not forget that there had been a "traitor" in their midst—or at least someone who was not on the side of Great Britain—in what must have been wartime. I was told that Craig was very reluctant to receive his degree from a "traitor," and only gave in to please the family members who wanted to see his graduation.

In memory of the chancellor, who did not long survive his naming to the post, the Euler family donated the Waterloo Lutheran University mace, which is a historic object in its own right, having been made by the last craftsman in Canada with the necessary skills and experience. (Dr. Overgaard has sent to the archives a correct version of the story of that symbol of our academic authority.) The other chancellors, Macdonald and Aird, were affable, impressive, and knew people who would be useful to us in Queen's Park and in Ottawa.

Honorary doctorates are bestowed for many reasons, perhaps most often for monetary favours universities have received or hope to receive. We had our share of those doctorates, many of them disappointing. I especially recall Lady Eaton who, after convocation, directed her chauffeur to the new Towers store in Waterloo, and on her arrival made a quick inspection of the outlet, one of the first of the chains that would finally become more than a threat to the old, family-run department stores. Lady Eaton was thus able to check out a competitor and receive a compliment with an honorary doctorate, while having no intention of enriching us to any financial degree.

A number of our early doctorates brought genuinely exceptional people to the campus, attracting the attention of the press, of course. Most exciting to my mind was Urho Kaleve Kekkonen, president of

Finland in the 1950s and 1960s. As head of the agrarian Centre Party, he had maintained a friendly neutrality with the USSR that had not been popular with a great many Finns. A review of the history of Finland, particularly since the First World War, suggests that there was good reason for the bad blood between Communist-supporting (Red) and non-Communist-supporting (White) Finns, which even in Canada had resulted in violent confrontations. (I recall that as a child I heard adults who were discussing an attack on a "hall," an ethnic gathering place, remark dismissively, "Those Finns again!") His visit to us must have been part of a longer trip of which I knew nothing except for a rumour that, because of fear of an attack on him by anti-Soviet Finnish Canadians, his appearance in a northern Ontario mining centre (Sudbury?) had been cancelled. Because I was situated quite close to him on the platform at convocation, I was aware that the several large men in the audience with bulges in their jackets under their left arms were probably ready to shoot anyone who might try to attack him, and that I would be in the line of fire. Of course nothing untoward happened.

Those convocations were held first in the Mutual Life Auditorium, and, as soon as it was available, in our own theatre-auditorium. (I seem to have a photo from Waterloo College days of a procession of the faculty and platform party to a Kitchener church, but we had long outgrown that location.) From the first, Waterloo Lutheran University tried for dignity and a bit of drama. Our convocations were stage-managed, in the beginning, by Jim Clark, the popular drama specialist and English professor, who added to our public image with his natural dignity and unfeigned affability, and in later years by colleagues equally versed in ceremonial observances. Suffice it to say, "We put on a good show."

I don't know how we managed to hire a military band for backup, perhaps through Professor Clark also being Major Clark of the Canadian Officers Training Corps (COTC). The leader was Derek Stannard, a young English bandsman. Am I wrong in recalling that he taught music to some of our students? He wrote a fanfare for one of our convocations. I have recently heard a colleague from those years recall the thrill as the players lifted their trumpets, decked with banners, and blew the first note. The same colleague recalled the excitement of walking in procession into the auditorium to the *March of the Gladiators*, which put us in timeless and exalted company.

The convocation ceremony combined ecclesiastical traditions (as was fitting since we were church related) and the usual academic rituals. After an invocation, students knelt to receive their degrees (their admission to the rank of graduate), then there was a hymn that could be sung by Christian, Muslim, or Jew without too much waffling about trinities or unities. More importantly, its intervals were suited to the vocal range of the ordinary congregation, not to mention the Lutherans who had not forgotten Bach or Luther himself. I have several pictures of one of these early assemblages in the theatre-auditorium. Most obvious is the colour displayed in the academic and military garb, and even in the fashionable dresses of the wives of faculty and administration, sitting in the front row. With that slight fear of making a misstep tightening the nerves, along with faith in Major Clark's confident control, the students and platform party felt they were participating in a significant rite.

In Waterloo Lutheran University's golden years we also gave doctorates to prominent politicians such as prime ministers Pearson and Diefenbaker. We recall George Hees with gratitude because until the Euler family gave us our own mace, he allowed us to borrow one from the Northwest Territories, a formidable object decorated with walrus teeth. The politician I remember best was Joey Smallwood, premier of Newfoundland. Our president, an American who refused to believe that Canadians were different, had imposed upon the Newfoundland premier a ban against any mention of politics in his address to us, which was like commanding a dog not to bark. Premier Smallwood began his speech by saying that he had been forbidden to speak of politics, so he had decided to talk about pigs. He then gave us a lively and informative account of his pig-farming operation—the audience chuckling inside at the joke because they suspected that the intensive and extensive pig farming *was* political, there being many opportunities in the Newfoundland of that day for using political trade-offs for concessions that made the pigs into valuable property: that is to say, discreet or not-so-discreet corruption existed. The listening faculty had a double treat: the unpopular, dictatorial president had been shown up, and the irrepressible premier was as entertaining as usual, "cocking a snook" at authority.

More sedate, at least in public, was Henry Astrup Larsen, who in 1940–42 had made the West to East journey through the Northwest Passage, with a second successful trip in the opposite direction in 1944. He was thus the first person to make the trip in a single season and the first to make it in both directions. I recall very little of his appearance at convocation, except that his presence reminded us that there were Lutherans of note outside of Waterloo County. His host for the visit recalls that the explorer's drink of choice was beer with aquavit as a chaser, and that he disposed of countless of those in an evening, which suggested that the cold northwest had given him a permanent chill to warm up. Was it that or the aquavit that carried him off at the early age of sixty-five?

Another honouree, Chester Ronning, brought a different view of Lutheran culture. He had been raised in China, a son of missionary parents, and retained his friendship with some of the Chinese leaders whom he had known in school days. We were shown a documentary of his life in which he was interviewed on a visit to China, sitting beside a friend who had risen to high rank in what must have then been Chairman Mao's government. Dr. Ronning was easy and affable, but his friend looked a bit constrained. The situation must have been delicate, given China's distrust of the West and its wish to be accepted among the nations. Dr. Ronning was at one time Canada's high commissioner in India. We were perhaps more honoured than he when we gave him our degree.

CHAPTER VIII

Other Visitors

A SMALL, CHURCH-RELATED UNIVERSITY could very soon become ingrown, especially if that church was seen by others as belonging to a minority, albeit a respected minority, in the larger society. From the beginning, the faculty and staff of Waterloo Lutheran University had included members of most groupings in Canada—with perhaps a higher representation of women than was usual. Because of missionary contacts, especially in Africa, Central America, and the Caribbean, we had students of various colours and cultures; these extraterritorial students helped to keep us from narrowness of interest or information.

Our chancellors and recipients of honorary degrees also kept us looking outwards, but in addition we had a number of strategies for bringing interesting people on campus. Quite early in our story, President Villaume entrusted the classics professor from Missouri with the responsibility for developing a lecture series. I hope there is some record of his achievements in the archives. I must confess that I do not recall any of the speakers he brought in, but I do remember that at the time we were impressed.

For years Dr. Overgaard ran a course in business with evening lectures by industrial, financial, and political leaders. Some of our recipients of honorary degrees participated in the course and became acquainted with our students in the process. The whole project was not only educational but a refined way of networking, with students gaining access to jobs and speakers discovering promising recruits for their enterprises.

It seemed clear to me that within the academic community the University of Waterloo was considered more prestigious (it certainly paid its professors better!), so I started an evening course in world literature that ran until I retired. I thought I could entice the public onto our campus to see for themselves how interesting Waterloo Lutheran University could be. I intended to run an evening course, open to visitors and well advertised, at which I could present lively speakers from our midst, as well as experts from elsewhere. The enterprise was a success. We filled our largest lecture hall with guests and students. Some of them came year after year. Students who had passed the course came back to audit the lectures as long as they were on campus because I regularly changed the topics, texts, and speakers. I tried to work around a different theme each year, and invited the whole faculty to suggest suitable books for study. Quite often a film, perhaps a foreign one, was substituted for a text so that students could compare the relative effectiveness of cinema and prose. For instance, in the series on Men and Women I used *Alfie*, a film that featured a charmer who was also a first-class cad. Was that the same series in which one of the history professors, born in France, lectured on *Madame Bovary* and confessed to me afterwards that it was the story of his mother?

When I chose Orwell's *Homage to Catalonia* as a text, someone was able to find for me a man who had fought in the Spanish Civil War and who recalled vividly his experiences as a raw recruit in the anti-Franco forces. By the time he gave the lecture for us, he had come to share Orwell's ambivalence towards some aspects of that struggle, thus helping students to see that political confrontations are rarely simple.

Towards the end, our registration dropped off. Perhaps I had lost touch with the times. Perhaps students no longer found it possible to read a book a week and participate in the small discussion group to which they had been assigned. These groups prepared a written report on at least one text, handed in the tape of a group meeting, and wrote mid-terms and final examinations. How would such students now find time for social interaction and sports, as well as part-time jobs? Since my retirement put an end to the course, that question is merely hypothetical, but I still think that the course was an education in itself.

I must confess that there were department chairmen who were not as pleased with the course as I was. The volunteers who gave the lectures—with persuasion—often put more time into their lectures for us than into some of their departmental duties. After all, it was flattering to appear before a mixed and admiring audience, to sip coffee at intermission with interested fans from the university community or the public, and to receive warm applause and a formal thank you at the end of the evening. Also, if they had researched their topics well, the lectures could be the bases for articles. I did resist the blandishments of the head of the University Press, Dr. Norman Wagner, who wanted to publish the lectures as a series. His lectures, usually on Hebrew or other Near Eastern texts, were exemplary, but some consisted more of enthusiasm than scholarship, and I did not want to have to winnow out the chaff. We had enough problems as it was.

In later years, speakers toured campuses, under various auspices such as the Canadian Authors Association. I do not recall how they came to us, but the two I remember most clearly were W.H. Auden, the poet, and Hugh MacLennan, the novelist. I had asked two young men from our English honours group to meet Auden at the airport. They watched disembarking passengers file by, but there was no sign of the great poet. At last it seemed that there was only a man in a long, much-worn military greatcoat, wearing red bedroom slippers. They took a chance, approached him and, yes, he was coming to Waterloo Lutheran University. All the way back he begged them to stop at a liquor store, but they felt it was wiser to deliver him to the campus in a sober state, so they saw him safely to the guest suite, and then got him what he wanted.

He arrived at the theatre-auditorium in what seemed to be a mood of acute disapproval. How had he been persuaded to come to this totally provincial place where he was met by humble students and now had to speak to probable illiterates? When I announced that we would have some music before the lecture, he looked even more bored. At that time we were fortunate in having as a student a soprano who had won the Rose Bowl competition in Toronto, and a director of music who enjoyed a challenge. They had rehearsed an aria from an opera for which Auden had done the libretto, and I settled down to watch the reaction of our guest. At the first notes he returned from wherever in his mind he had taken refuge, and listened with care to the competent rendition of his and the composer's work. His lecture was, I hope, delivered with more warmth because of his surprise at hearing that we also knew Stravinsky, and in our midst he was not cut off from civilization. (He still wore his red slippers.)

Hugh MacLennan liked us from the beginning. To meet him I had dispatched a charming faculty member from psychology and a young male lecturer who at that time was her admirer. Like the poet, MacLennan was interested in the liquor store. After dinner the young people delivered him to me in the old music room, which was full of people who probably hoped to hear more about *Two Solitudes*. A glance told me that MacLennan was standing up only because he was supported on either side. He was somehow conducted to a seat in the front row, and on the way managed to say, "I'll be all right. Keep talking until I give you the nod." The audience must have wondered what had happened to me. Usually I am very brief on such occasions, but here I was havering on about novels, Montreal, Cape Breton, the weather.... At last he nodded and I could say, "I now introduce the distinguished novelist, etc." And he stood up, albeit carefully, and remained upright while he delivered a witty address.

When it was time to get him back to the railway station, his minders were exhausted, if charmed. They made affectionate farewells, the steward helped him up the steps, and as the train started he cried, "No, I won't leave," and tried to jump down. Somehow he was restrained, and disappeared to the east. We heard later that now and again he would get lost, and had turned up at one time in California, wondering how he had got there. The whole experience had some effect on the way I presented his works to students. From his novels I had gathered that the author was a steady, not to mention dull, product of a narrow, Presbyterian Maritime culture. The individual we entertained was anything but.

From day to day I do not think that we ever stopped to reflect on the diversity of our faculty and student body because we had somehow all melded, held together by the academic routine and the local geography, the streets, the shops, the gossip. We would be reminded of the wider world when we talked of holiday plans or when some event would open a view out of the country, as when a Finnish professor of religion and culture was summoned home to the funeral of the composer Sibelius—at least that was what was whispered. He and the family never spoke of it.

We had several Estonian colleagues. During the time of Waterloo Lutheran University, they were unable to visit their homeland, but after the Cold War they were welcome there. As an older one said, "I was an honoured guest at a state dinner where formerly they would have had me shot." A younger professor was in the middle of the negotiations and initiatives that gave Estonia its independence. I have remarked upon the diversity of our student body, one aspect of which deserves special mention. Two of our business professors, Dr. Overgaard and Dr. Bonner, in association with a federal body that encouraged development abroad (CIDA), began a course for overseas students who were chosen by their own government and maintained for a period of time on our campus. They also visited corporations and industries from which they could learn how to develop financial and industrial entities in their own countries. All this involved a close rapprochement with the governments concerned. Not only did we gain unusual students but our faculty became more exotic. Dr. Bonner came back from his conferences with African rulers carrying a chief's regalia, including symbolic fly-whisk, which he modelled for our edification at some faculty gathering. He also brought back a bush baby that he had been given. When his son-in-law developed a tropical disease, it appeared that exoticism could be carried too far. I am afraid I have heard that Dr. Bonner's files are sealed in the archives. Surely someone will be able to gain access to them to chronicle a very interesting venture in Waterloo Lutheran

University's history, and in the story of Canadian–overseas relations. It seems that the only disadvantage of the whole scheme was that the visiting students did not all want to go home. As a result, I heard that CIDA decided it was better for us to send instructors abroad than to bring students to Canada.

The anecdote from that time that stands out the most in my mind, however, is the story of Dr. Overgaard having to telephone the federal minister in charge to say that an African princess was having a miscarriage—and what were we to do? Since she was a married woman, no scandal was involved, but we felt it would be better to keep it out of the papers. I gather that Paul Martin Sr. advised us to maintain silence, and everything turned out for the best.

The Overgaard–Bonner program for overseas students had a corollary that connected it to the English curriculum. Among our innovations was a course with an unwieldy name, something like "Literature in English Other Than British, American, or Canadian." Someone—Dr. Margaret Allen, I believe—suggested the title "English Literature of the Diaspora," which I wish I had had the courage to use, but I finally gave in and called it "Commonwealth Literature," as did the very few other universities who had ventured outside of the conventional canon of texts at that time. South Africa had by then left the Commonwealth, however, and other former colonies were moving towards or had reached independence.

Dr. Bonner was very interested in the course, and told the representatives of overseas governments about it, when he was persuading them to send students to us. He was carried away a bit when he praised it to Tom Mboya in Kenya, and told him that I had used one of his books as a required text. When Dr. Bonner reported back to me, I felt I had to make it true, so I hurriedly put in orders for the book and appended it to our list of suggested readings. When I heard about Mboya's assassination in 1969 I felt that we had lost a friend, or at least an acquaintance.

I add a further comment. My relationship with the University of Aberdeen was through Professor Lothian, who had been head of the English Department at the University of Saskatchewan. He and his wife welcomed me to Aberdeen where they had settled after the war. They were then mourning the death of their son in a plane crash in Africa. Tom Mboya and the son, who was some sort of British representative in Africa, had become close. Tom had said goodbye to him as he left on the fatal flight and then had taken his friend's wife and children to another plane that would return them to Scotland. The Lothians, grieving for their son in the early 1960s, had further to lament the loss of his friend in 1969. True, none of this concerns Waterloo Lutheran University except through myself, but it demonstrates that university frontiers are not fixed and that a small Lutheran institution could have wide-ranging connections.

Left Flora Roy with the first volume of her *Recollections;* *bottom* Dr. Glen Carroll, in a typical teaching stance.

Left Gwen Mitches crowns Kathy Burrows in a Queen's Pageant, 1960s; *bottom* Don Morgenson as a young professor.

Left Tamara Giesbrecht, registrar; *bottom* left to right—Jane Campbell, Gerry Noonan, Flora Roy, Charlotte Cox. Photograph courtesy of Paul Tiessen.

Frosh, 1947. Photograph courtesy of the *Record*.

Top Eileen Stumpf, the "coffee lady"; *bottom* Mary Kay Lane, teaching in academic robes in the 1960s.

Top Flora Roy with Dr. Delton Glebe; *bottom* Tom Ramautarsingh with Flora Roy, Homecoming Week, September 1995.

Top left Jim Clarke, Flora Roy's teaching associate in the English Department; *top right* Helen Forler from the Registrar's Office; *bottom* Security services.

Willi Nassau of Audiovisual Services with his model train.

Left Dr. William Villaume, president of Waterloo Lutheran University; *bottom* Dr. Frank Peters, president of Wilfrid Laurier University, 1968–78.

Flora Roy receiving an honourary degree from Wilfrid Laurier University.
Maureen Forrester, left, was Chancellor of the university at that time.

CHAPTER IX

Academic Relations

A s WATERLOO COLLEGE, we had strong academic ties to the University of Western Ontario, where our curriculum was set, texts chosen, and faculty approved. The examinations, too, were composed at Western and the honours papers were marked there; general papers could be called in for evaluation too, though I do not recall that happening in my time at the college.

In *Recollections of Waterloo College* I referred briefly to an incident affecting our English Department that perhaps I should describe again. One of our lecturers, who had been in the armed forces (chiefly in London, if my recollections are correct), was scornful of everything that Western respected, and made his disapproval obvious. He would have preferred a freewheeling approach to university teaching: individual choice of texts and interpretation, with condemnation of almost everything in the canon of that time. At a meeting of the Senate of Western it was resolved that his contract should not be renewed. Our dean who, I think, was becoming weary of our being a mere subsidiary of Western, was willing to fight the order. I refused to back him. In good conscience I could not say that he was an ornament to the kind of university we were hoping to create.

The campus faculty association seized on the matter at once and made it an issue of academic freedom, since the member concerned was openly dismissive of Christianity along with other bourgeois pieties that he associated with a church college. They tried to arouse other faculty associations in order to have Waterloo College put under an interdict such as the one that had almost destroyed United College in Winnipeg. This action involved Western, where the proposal to dismiss the rebel had originated—and, behold, the motion disappeared from the minutes of the Western Senate, leaving Waterloo College with the full blame. Fortunately for us, the academic year was ending, and faculty members would be off to enjoy their long summer vacations (things *were* different in those days). The matter was dropped. I never felt that the faculty member at the centre had much interest in being a celebrity, which the media tried to make him—and I also guessed that the public was not ready to get excited about a new "Crowe" case like that in Winnipeg (see chap. 15). At Waterloo College, which was on the verge of turning into Waterloo Lutheran University, other concerns took our attention and our first crisis faded away. I have not forgotten, however, that Western had caused the problem because they had taken seriously their responsibility for standards in the affiliated institutions. One of my students from Waterloo College days told me fairly recently that after some of my English lectures she and her orthodox friends would say, "And she still goes to church!" I never heard any negative comments from the administration, was never challenged by my students. At the time I presented the texts as honestly and openly as possible, with well-reasoned arguments and up-to-date research. That was how we all treated English literature in those halcyon days.

While the influence of the University of Western Ontario was strongest because of our formal relation to them, we were all shaped by our own undergraduate and graduate universities; in the English Department this largely meant the University of Toronto which, at the time, was struggling to hold its own against ambitious American competitors. I am writing of the era just before Northrop Frye and Marshall McLuhan put Toronto on the academic map. I am not sure that the faculty there felt they were best represented by those two darlings of the media, but such scholars did a lot for the image of the university. My own chief influences at the University of Toronto had been A.S.P. Woodhouse and F.E.L. Priestley, who were erudite, combative, and balanced. I realize now that financial problems were making it difficult to hire the big names who would have captured academic attention.

Our contacts with British academic thought were minimal. It was some time before the pronouncements of the Leavises had influence. We were aware of William Empson's denunciation of Milton, and of his seven types of ambiguity. C.S. Lewis and D.H. Lawrence were read perhaps for their entertainment value, as much as for their opinions of Milton or Whitman, while there were people who still secretly read Bradley on Shakespeare and even Dowden.

The burgeoning of critical quarterlies and other journals was soon to come, as the financial climate made it possible. The yearly conference of the Learned Societies of Canada expanded and spawned international conferences such as the Lowry Symposium of 1997 in Toronto, with leading speakers from New Zealand and the United States. In our golden years we certainly felt the excitement of combative scholarship.

CHAPTER X

The English Curriculum

———— ✦ ————

WHEN WE BECAME INDEPENDENT OF WESTERN, we had in place a curriculum and an academic program that we could modify in time into an educational framework that would embody the intentions of the faculty, administration, and board of a new university. We did not have to lose time in defining our mission and working out all the details of standards, procedures, and appeals. Students already in courses proceeded to graduation; new recruits could look forward to graduating under the same rules as those in effect when they enrolled. But of course there were changes, and sometimes as we tried to proceed under new regulations, we found ourselves running two sets of courses until at last everyone was on the same schedule. This meant extra classes—taught without any extra remuneration. There were years when we gave only the first-year honours courses in English, and all the honours students took them together. This initially terrified first-year students in the general English program, but soon they gained maturity and assurance from close contact with their elders. The courses were equally demanding: there was no "dumbing down" nor any concession—perhaps I should say no compassion—but the system produced first-rate graduates. As we added faculty and registrants, we were bit by bit able to sort the students into their proper stages and we gave all four years of honours in each academic year, but I felt that we lost something. The intellectual competition had been trying when fresh persons mingled with fourth-year students, but I never felt that there was any personal denigration of the newcomers, and friendships developed across academic boundaries.

We tried to avoid the stratagem of putting general and honours students into the same classes, and assigning more reading and written work for those designated as honours. From the first we accepted Western's approach that the general and honours programs were quite different. In time I think we evolved a more interesting general program than that of Western. We asked general students majoring in English to take three mandatory courses that would give them some familiarity with the canon of English literature, arranged chronologically, and in addition they could choose the rest of their major courses from an extensive and interesting list, including American, Canadian, and Commonwealth texts. The choice could not be as wide for students who were hoping to get their degrees in evening and summer school classes, but even they had more choice than general students at the University of Toronto. We tried to make it clear that the general English student was not doing an easier program than was the honours English student, but one better suited to someone who did not intend to pursue graduate work in English literature.

Students in general English who decided they wanted to go on to further degrees in the subject were encouraged to take a fourth year of study of honours English courses that would fill in areas of the subject that they would need for qualifying examinations for graduate work. As time went on, and government funding depended on registration, the qualifying examinations became less important; I seem to recall that they were dropped for an MA. In the old days, if students were accepted into an MA program with some deficiencies in coursework, they were required to correct them by taking the appropriate undergraduate courses.

Though we had inherited our curriculum from Western, as I have noted before, most of us were fresh from graduate school in Toronto, bringing with us a conviction that the organization of a department's courses mattered. Honours English graduates from Toronto were going out into the world to uphold the reputation of the discipline, usually to teach in English departments in high schools and, to some extent, in universities. R.D. McMaster, discussing scholarship at the University of Toronto, stated: "that decade was a flowering of admirable tendencies that had been maturing in Toronto for over half a century and that would within less than another decade be wrecked and swept aside by Maoism, bigness, and business efficiency."[1] But though the Toronto honours English program was "wrecked and swept aside," its influence continued in places like Waterloo Lutheran University and survived into the era after 1973. Sometime between 1976 and 1978, Dr. F.E.L. Priestley was asked to report (to the Canada Council?) on the various English curricula of universities—was it just in Ontario or in Canada? He spoke at a Learned Societies gathering in 1977 or 1978 on the subject, indicating that all was well. (In his earlier report he had praised the program at Waterloo Lutheran University, implying that we had lost little of what Toronto had offered in its best time.) The English professor who was to become my successor rose to declare that the speaker was deluding himself; the world of English academia had changed, and Dr. Priestley hadn't noticed. The objector didn't specify what the changes involved, but when he became head of the English Department at Waterloo Lutheran University it was obvious that he was a convert to deconstruction and intended to make it the philosophy behind all departmental alterations.

Before continuing, I must make it clear that from my final day in office as chair I kept myself aloof from the politics of the English Department, and not until my successor's removal did I have any idea of what had been going on. I believe that some in the university thought of our department as being rather lax in discipline. Actually, the department was made up of strong-minded individuals who let me run the show as long as they could depend on being left to develop their courses and their research as they liked. If I had stepped out of line, they would have deposed me—perhaps with regret, but with finality. I was not surprised to learn that when my successor started to take steps towards purging the place of old-fashioned academics and replacing them with new types of university teachers, they organized a no-confidence vote: they had uncovered evidence of what would now be called sexual harassment. Rumours surfaced that a concerned parent had contacted the dean to express disbelief that such behaviour was being overlooked or accepted. This intervention was, I believe, what persuaded the administration to allow the deposition to go through. The reader might like to know that the ousted department chair then got a job at an important American university and before long reported to the *Journal of American Chairmen in English* that he was well on his way to cleaning his new department of those devoted to out-of-date scholarship. His new colleagues must have been more docile or less well organized. At Waterloo Lutheran University there was in time a healthy adoption of some of the new terminology, and of many of the new approaches to post-secondary English—for instance, the introduction of a program in women's studies—but generally the revolution passed us over, leaving what seemed to be a balanced curriculum. I will not go into details because a researcher can find the evidence of these changes in successive university calendars.

Note

1 R.D. McMaster, rev. of *English Studies in Toronto*, by Robin S. Harris, *English Studies in Canada*, 14.3 (September 1988).

CHAPTER XI

New Programs

W E MAY HAVE BEEN CONSERVATIVE in that we kept a good deal of the canon in our curriculum, and we may have remained centred on the texts themselves rather than on trends or causes for which they could be used as illustrations, negative or positive, but we may also have been one of the more controversial English Departments in Canada because of our innovations. I know that our own academic councils and Senate sometimes found it hard to believe that some of our additions to or modifications of orthodox programs could find a place in a university. Among these were film studies, writing, and in time the interdisciplinary major in communication studies.

I am not sure that we were the first to get all three courses in running order. Film studies has expanded since my time, writing has been given up, chiefly because of administration concerns about funds, and the communication studies area now has several hundred majors.

Constructive changes in the department were based on two main considerations: (1) What would keep us abreast of other universities, not only in Canada and the US? I followed trends closely through MLA publications, the newsletter of heads of English Departments in the US and Canada, the *Higher Education Supplement* of the *Times* of London, and various individual books, including one on the concept of honours programs as distinct from general. The Learned Societies' meetings kept me in touch with academics in Canada, and I cultivated my university acquaintances in Ireland, Scotland, and England. When the young Dean of Women at Trinity College, Dublin, recalled that a relative of mine had once been her fellow student, she accepted me as part of the university family—and my friends, the Lothians, gave me an entré to the University in Aberdeen and through that to ones in Edinbugh and St Andrews; and (2) concern about the future of higher education. If finances became tight, taxpayers and donors might start to specify the purposes for which universities might use their money. I felt we should always be prepared with evidence to demonstrate that English departments were useful as well as life-enhancing. I recall a meeting in Toronto at which older professors gave impassioned speeches declaring that when they lectured to students on Shakespeare, and so forth, the students were getting ample training in such practical matters as communication. I am sure that the students were being led to enjoy the texts along with the inspiring lectures, but I wasn't sure that every taxpayer would feel it was all worth the cost. As it turned out, I was wrong then, but as I write I can see my fears from the late 1960s and the 1970s becoming real threats against academic freedom.

Dr. Paul Tiessen, who did his graduate research in film studies, is writing the history of his specialty in our department, and so I am able to direct the researcher to his version, which will be based on documents as well as on memory. I will only recount what I recall personally about the introduction of the cinema into our departmental offerings. My recollections are not as detailed as I would wish, but I do remember that from an early stage we used film as a support for literature, especially in teaching Shakespeare. In my world literature course I tried to introduce at least one film a year. Russian films based on the classics made books like Dostoevsky's *The Idiot* come alive, offsetting the effect of some insensitive translations—or even of the unfamiliar forms of address in Russian novels. But it was a different matter to introduce our students to the study of film as an art and to bring out the ways in which it both related to book literature and differed from it. Because I retired before film studies reached maturity on campus, I have had no opportunity to judge the effect each form might have had on the other. Would an

understanding of film enhance the students' judgments of literature, or vice versa? One thing I have been told: beginners in our
current program in film studies are much more aware of critical
approaches to the medium, an awareness that may come from the
sophistication of courses on film in the high schools, where teachers have been well prepared for such programs.

Our ventures into the serious teaching of writing were, I think,
successful in teaching students how to write academic papers and
basically how to develop words into sentences and sentences into
paragraphs, but we were always under attack because we were teaching material that should have been covered in elementary and secondary education. It was obvious that a great many university students had little skill in handling the English language. This was
not a new phenomenon. As a graduate student in Saskatoon, I had
been hired to teach a non-credit course in writing; the students
were selected by professors who had noted their incompetence. In
those days the local newspaper reported the examination results of
each course at the university, thus at the end of the year I was able
to discover the standing of my students, and was surprised, but
pleased to note, that they had done very well. The department head
had introduced the course as an experiment and felt that he had
been vindicated in the eyes of his colleagues who thought that writing skills should have been acquired earlier.

When I got to Ontario, I found that the universities of Toronto
and Western Ontario, at least, gave required courses in writing. I
gather that they were controversial, and in time they were phased
out. I had no doubt that they were helpful—and for some students
necessary. For a few years Waterloo Lutheran University had a quick
proficiency examination for students: under supervision, they wrote
a short essay on one of a variety of suggested topics. Their papers
were then divided among volunteers from all departments who were
asked to spot unsatisfactory performances. (Involving all departments was a political move, because unless they saw with their
own eyes the need for training, they would not support our plans.)
At first the students so identified were assigned to members of the
English Department for coaching, but very soon, it was clear that we
were imposing a heavy burden on already overworked faculty. I felt

the only solution was to hire the necessary instructors and offer regular courses for students who required them.

But should writing courses be for credit? They required time and continued effort on the part of students as well as faculty, and thus cut into the time they should have devoted to credit courses. Giving credit—but only when improvement was noticeable in all aspects of academic writing—seemed to me the only answer. There were few if any objectors in our faculty or administration, and I suspect that the English Department would even today still have a similar program if the funds were available.

After my retirement a committee was formed by the administration to consider the problem of writing assistance, and it recommended that there should be a resource person to whom students in need of help could be referred. That was better than nothing, but I never found it very satisfactory. The basic reason was that the approach was negative. It began by identifying the student as substandard. The approach was to correct errors as they appeared—or perhaps to give classes on common errors. That was the conventional approach, but there was a better one.

The course I gave in Saskatchewan was based on two texts—the loss of which I deeply regretted. (I had to return my copies to the department head at the end of the year and have even forgotten their titles.) Their approach was to have the student make complete statements on a subject, then help him (mine were all male) to see that his statements related to one another and could be arranged to lead the reader through one part of a discussion—thus, we had a paragraph. The paragraphs in turn had a connection to one another and properly arranged would make an essay. One could have given a very old-fashioned course in rhetoric (say, of the sixteenth century), and some pioneers were doing just that in the US, but twentieth-century students—at least the ones I knew—were likely to be put off by scholastic terminology.

When we started our writing program at Waterloo Lutheran University we were very fortunate in having in the department an instructor who was sharply intelligent on her own, but who could see into the minds of less bright mortals and try to help them bring out their potential. Poor as we were, we found enough money to send her to a summer course—Oklahoma, I think, because that was a centre for the approach I favoured, though I think there were also exciting experiments in Salt Lake City.

We also hired the wife of a science professor at the University of Waterloo who had some experience in the teaching of writing and was enthusiastic about our intentions. When her husband returned to the US, she left, too, but told me she was proceeding to a doctorate there in the teaching of writing.

Our remedial writing venture was a tremendous success. Though we still took only students who were selected from our proficiency test, we made it clear that they were the fortunate ones, and the students begging to be allowed to register underlined that approach. (Of course some thought it would be an easy way to get a credit!) We also had sections for ESL students who were even more highly motivated, and all worked hard, as did the faculty. I felt that we had a major academic success story—if only we could have continued. There were two problems: finding suitable instructors and sufficient money. After I retired, I think there was an offshoot into private enterprise. Many people were happy to pay a tutorial firm for improvement in their ability to communicate. Perhaps that is the way to go, as long as others do not actually write essays for students—but that is the story of another type of enterprise that has been with us for a very long time, and for which I do not see an end.

At our neighbouring university, the problem of student writing was being handled in quite a different way. At first I heard no echoes from our ventures in teaching writing, but a new chair was brought in to the University of Waterloo from the West who at once went on the attack, announcing at a meeting of provincial English chairs that my approach was not the right one. His idea was to blame the teachers in elementary and secondary schools, and he and an aide (who became the spokesperson) set out to arouse public indignation about the poor job being done by the schools. My reply was that *we* had trained those teachers; showing any contempt for the teaching of writing was not inspiring them to do a better job.

Here I can go back to my roots for an example. Saskatchewan had been in the forefront of educational reform, and in the 1930s its schools had become much more in line with the modern approach to teaching, emanating especially from Columbia Teachers College in New York, than were schools in Ontario. I was told that sometime in that era a deputation of high school teachers had called on the head of the English Department at the University of Saskatchewan, where they told him that he and his colleagues had had all the fun of teaching English up to that time while avoiding dreary aspects, such as grammar and composition. The teachers were going to turn the tables. They would have fun, and the professors would have to deal with the results. I do not know if that meeting had anything to do with me being hired, among others, to give the University of Saskatchewan's first courses in writing. I do not assume that all high school teachers gave up on grammar and composition, but I know that there were students who came through the education mill with no concept of a sentence. In fact, I have seen essays several pages long in which there was not a single punctuation mark. No, this had nothing to do with James Joyce, or the unconscious, or stream of consciousness. The essay was supposed to be plain, discursive prose. You can see why I felt that a completely new beginning was needed if we were to rescue the language.

When I pointed out that there was nowhere for our teachers to learn how to teach writing—or even to learn what constituted acceptable writing—I was told by my opponents that they should have learned that at Teachers College, which only suggested that the speakers knew little about Teachers College: there wasn't enough space in the curriculum after studying issues such as the legally imposed rights and obligations of school boards, principals, and teachers.

Our instructors in writing got in touch with those in English literature in our regional centre for education and tried to work on improving the situation in co-operation with the teachers instead of castigating them. Out of that collaboration came a weekend of seminars on writing instruction, ending with a huge general meeting chaired by one of our graduates, Tom Ramautarsingh (later Dr. Thompson Ramautarsingh). He organized similar gatherings for some time until, as might be expected, the subject became politicized in struggles between governments and parties, and communication took a back seat. Those meetings were largely sponsored by elementary and secondary school teachers, but we had one of our own, bringing in a couple of American speakers who were very enthusiastic about the positive approach to teaching writing, and they encouraged us in our intentions. We had also invited as a speaker one of our graduates who was facing the same problems as a faculty member at the University of Alberta. All this widened the approach to the problem and got it away from the local standoff of Waterloo Lutheran University against the University of Waterloo. The result? I am not sure that written communication has improved, though its oral equivalent has. The computer keyboard, the spell-check, and the grammar checker do not seem to have made current prose any more accessible—in fact, often it seems less so.

Though I suggested earlier that anyone who wants a detailed study of film studies on campus should consult Paul Tiessen's work on the subject, I will include some information to support my claim that our program was really innovative. The credit should go to the first director, but first some history.

I suggested earlier that in the 1960s we felt that we were in competition with the University of Waterloo, not in science, and of course not in engineering, but in the arts. When we got our charter, we were already running a respectable arts program, and I remind the reader that at our last convocation as part of Western the majority of the gold medals in English were won by students from Waterloo College. We had been thinking about introducing film, and I was so rash as to mention it at a meeting where an administrator from the University of Waterloo was present. Very soon after, our competitors announced that they were introducing film studies, and they quickly hired a couple of experts from Czechoslovakia. I had been hesitant in announcing our plans because we hadn't found the person who would have to be all things: technician, administrator, lecturer, public relations expert, and film fanatic. We eventually found him, and in spite of the advantage in time that our friends "down the road" had, we were soon in the running.

A short time ago, I was discussing the history of film at Waterloo Lutheran University with the first director, Willi Nassau. I recalled that he and his wife arrived for an interview with their rough-haired dachshund, Maxi (later replaced by Nepomuk, named after the patron saint of Bohemia, from whence his master's family had long ago migrated to Vienna). Willi and Hermine (from Graz) brought another exotic shade to our already multi-hued campus. Willi reminded me that he had also brought his model Austrian railroad, which must have been lodged at the time in his van. It was not long before campus characters of all types were helping him with it, which meant adjusting switches, cleaning rails, and running its carriages around. Willi did not confine his interests in transport to rail: he had been a glider pilot, he was an ardent sailor, and he loved cars. What had that to do with developing and running a film studies course?

In the first place I knew that we could not afford to pay a full salary for just the teaching of film, but Waterloo Lutheran University needed someone to organize audiovisual aids, to centralize them, and to arrange for their maintenance, repair, and provenance. At the time each department went its own way. Thus someone who was a professional photographer like Willie, but who had a technical side, and could repair, improvise, and invent, would be invaluable. Of course there was opposition to the move to take projectors and other equipment away from the control of individual departments, but most chairmen saw the advantages in having someone else deal with maintenance and surveillance. (Projectors somehow migrated to rec rooms and didn't come back.) One department, especially, ignored all moves toward centralization, and when it moved to another building, its clandestine hoard came to light, mostly quite useless stuff—at least in the eyes of the Audiovisual Department.

Where could we put such a department initially? The English Department had offices in houses on Albert Street, later torn down (and none too soon). In the basement of one we had a classroom, and nearby what might have been a storage room. That became our AV centre. Willi moved in and installed his own equipment, along with the very little that the university owned, and we were off. As I look back, I cannot believe that he gave courses, built up a staff, acquired equipment by various wheelings and dealings, and networked with people doing similar jobs (but with much more financial support) elsewhere in Canada and the US, and across the Atlantic.

When Willi's widowed mother gave up on trying to manage her wild son, she entrusted him to the Jesuits, though he was a Lutheran. The priests supplemented his sharp and inquisitive mind with a very good general education. He later joined the Allied forces in Italy as a photographer. From there he moved north with the troops, anticipating always a welcome from the local *fräuleins* who were impressed by the uniforms and jeeps of their liberators, as he once told me. At his job interview, he showed us slides of his more serious photographic endeavours, including one of the wheel of a train. The railroad aficionado demonstrated an aesthetic eye, as well as a critical one.

When I saw him recently, Willi reminded me that his pastor in Ottawa was responsible for his coming to us. But how did he get to Ottawa? Perhaps that and other mysteries will be explained if he writes an autobiography, as I have begged him to do. All I know is that he had been working for the National Film Board and was "resting" because he had overspent his budget. Then, for his pastor, he gave a talk on film for a young people's church group. Our Dr. Overgaard, who knew I was looking for just the right person for our program, happened to see the presentation and was impressed. Thence came the invitation to an interview and the subsequent hiring.

Eventually, I hope to write of the building of a fine arts program on campus, but here I will only mention that, since we felt that film belonged in such a program, we had one more reason to hire someone who was an expert. In his sometimes misspent youth, Willi had seen as many films as possible, not knowing that later he would lecture on the history of cinema.

Later in his career with us, Willi revealed an interest in museums. I learned that as a youngster he had virtually haunted the museums in Vienna. On campus he built up a collection of photographs and projection equipment, and when ordered to clear it out, presented it on our behalf to the National Museum in Ottawa, leaving only a few choice items at the university. These are now and again lent to various shows and exhibitions. (My Minox camera is another item left here. I think there is one other in Canada. Also, my Minox projector is unique.) Before he returned, Willi had forged links for us with the Corning Glass Museum in New York State, and with a museum in Alberta. More recently he was involved with the Canadian Clay and Glass Gallery in Waterloo and with a similar institution in Austria that he may have helped to establish.

CHAPTER XII

Interdepartmental Majors

I N THIS CHAPTER I PROPOSE TO DEAL LARGELY with further innovations, concentrating on our interdepartmental majors, but first I
want to reiterate that our concept of a good education included a
comprehensive introduction to the fine arts. I hope someone will
write the story of music on campus, from the founding of the Faculty of Music, and its later home, the Aird Building with its Maureen
Forrester Hall.

I cannot give a full and accurate history of the visual arts, especially drawing and painting, and printmaking, along with art appre-
ciation, but I do know something about how the fine arts program
came to be. When I arrived, I soon met the bursar and artist Ned
Cleghorn, father of former chancellor of Wilfrid Laurier and retired
CEO of the Royal Bank of Canada, John E. Cleghorn, who at that
time was an obstreperous youngster, the mascot of the college football team, and the terror of the university president's children who
lived on campus. The Cleghorns lived just across Albert Street in
easy proximity to whatever was going on.

Hazel Cleghorn came from an old Waterloo County family,
which may explain how she and Ned found themselves attached
to Waterloo College. She was bright, helpful, energetic, and hos-
pitable, and devoted to drama as represented by the K-W Drama
Society. Ned was efficient in his job, but probably most interested in
teaching art. Since his office was close to mine, I became well ac-

quainted with our resident artist, who was a delightful raconteur with a whimsical, self-deprecating sense of humour. I gathered that he came from "old-family" Montreal. His father had decreed that if he wanted to be an artist he must first train in business administration. Remember that in those days "real men" didn't go out sketching nature; that was mostly an avocation of English ladies or their colonial imitators, or of a few bohemian characters one did not associate with socially.

Having acquired his business training, Ned, I gather, began living in an area populated with impecunious young artists and writers. I recall that he once told me how he and Abe Klein transported a bed by hand across Montreal, the story enlivened by chuckles at how that would have looked to anyone of his parents' class who might have spotted the procession. His "partner in crime" was, of course, A.M. Klein, the distinguished poet.

After Ned Cleghorn left us to take up a position at the Montreal Museum of Art, our campus had a period devoid of fine arts. I do not know how the program was restored, but its story illustrates an unusual degree of departmental co-operation and was a precursor to the development of interdepartmental majors though, strictly speaking, art was not one of them.

Perhaps the idea started in one of the excited discussions we used to have in the faculty lounge, where, as we ate lunch or sipped coffee, we vied with each other in tearing down and rebuilding "this sorry scheme of things entire." A few of us were sent off to find out which members of the faculty were interested in the fine arts, with the possibility of starting a program. The scheme came to centre on the History Department, where we could find people knowledgeable about various historical periods. We sketched out a course on the history of art (mostly painting), and we found faculty members from various departments who had special interests in artists: ancient, medieval, Italian, Flemish, French, and so on. I didn't give any lectures, but I organized the schedule, created the examinations from questions submitted by the lecturers, and arranged for marking of papers. I must admit that I exercised editorial discretion in regard to marks, and brought the various evaluations into some kind of balance.

The course was a great success. Lecturers enjoyed conveying their enthusiasm for their own infatuations. More and more, Dr. Paape of the History Department assumed responsibility for this course, and when I returned from research one fall he was able to tell me that he had found someone to take over the course, a Dr. Ilse Friesen from Vienna, whose husband taught art at Guelph. She worked for us part-time for twelve years before she became a full-time professor.

Dr. Friesen was not the first person hired specifically for art after the era of Ned Cleghorn. In 1971 Michal Manson was first appointed as a sort of artist in residence. (She became a full-time instructor in 1975 and at last got tenure in 1989.) She was supposed to arrange art exhibitions on campus and to teach drawing and painting as part of the aesthetics course given by Professor Robert Langen of the Philosophy Department. She recalls that she reported to the dean of arts, as well as to Professor Langen.

Michal reminded me that before she came Paul Fournier was artist in residence, and that there may have been others between him and Ned Cleghorn. The position could not have been very remunerative because Michal also taught at Conestoga College. When she was hired full-time by Waterloo Lutheran College, she gave three courses, two in drawing, one in painting. When the interdepartmental program in fine arts evolved, she reported to the chairperson of the Fine Arts Committee, among whom were Michael Ballin and Ira Ashcroft. When Ilse Friesen was hired, she became chair or coordinator of the committee.

Once a year, in those early days, fine arts became a visible part of the campus when Michal Manson organized the "clothesline" show of art work by students. She started the show to give the students a chance to make some extra money, but the rows of paintings and drawings pinned to lines strung across the big foyer of the arts building had another result. It put art in the middle of student life and probably attracted more students to the program than any advertising campaign could have. The clothesline shows stopped when the Robert Langen Art Gallery was opened.

If the staffing of the fine arts program was a bit informal, the siting of the classes was even more so. For a time the students drew

and painted in the basement of the library, then in an ordinary classroom in the arts building. Michal Manson recalls the nude model
posing on a desk at the front of the room, and the students sitting at
the usual classroom desks as they tried to capture her curves and
lines. Later the classes were moved to a house on Bricker Avenue,
which, one assumes, would be less public as well as less draughty.

What I have written here is very much subject to correction,
and I am hoping that Robert Langen may see fit to contribute his
own more accurate interpretation of the founding and growth of
fine arts to the archives, though his story may relate more to the history of Wilfrid Laurier University rather than that of Waterloo
Lutheran University. Professor Langen reminded me, for instance,
that very early in our history as an independent university, Dr. Villaume had instituted a Cultural Affairs Committee with responsibility for fostering the arts—or more specifically, music, art, drama,
dance, creative writing, and so on. I wish to give credit to him here:
first, for his belief that the impractical aspects could not be left out
of an educational ambience; second, for establishing a definite
committee with a head who was required to answer for its actions;
and last, for giving the committee a budget. Professor Robert Alexan-
der had been chosen to head the committee. Dr. Villaume had little
faith in Canadians, so he had chosen a fellow American, but a mod-
est one who felt that he didn't know enough about the field and
hence asked Professor Langen, with an interest in aesthetics, to help
him. They decided to hire artists to be a presence on campus and in
time to give instruction that could be made part of the aesthetics
courses. Paul Fournier was their first choice for artist in residence,
and though he was going through a difficult time personally, the
appointment did what was needed. Little by little, the field was
extended and we found ourselves with an art program. Professor
Langen also reminded me of the many achievements of the Cultural Affairs Committee, among them the art history courses given
abroad in the summers, the visit of the Winnipeg Ballet, and the
twentieth-century art show in the new women's residence.

Fine arts became a sort of interdepartmental operation by hazard,
but the others were planned, though their stories were more origi-

nal and fortuitous than the word planned might suggest. Before I try to reconstruct the process of building them, I should once more mention the unusual amity on our early campus or it would be hard to believe that so much co-operative effort could have been volunteered by so many people of diverse interests and intentions. For instance, we had the History Department sponsoring art history in a program that offered a course in design, whose godfather was the School of Business. Of course there were differences of opinion and much arguing in committees since we were all human. (A committee of robots has not yet been invented.) One interdepartmental program—communication studies—got under way more slowly than the others because it offered more challenge to entrenched "ideas of a university," but it, too, finally took off.

One of our presidents may have been just a bit too subject to suggestion for his own good. Back in Toronto, where he had come from to be our head of French and Spanish, his old friends took considerable interest in his career as president of a new university, and they tested ideas on him that could not at that time be introduced into an institution as rigid as the University of Toronto had become. The suggestion that appealed to him most was that he should turn Waterloo Lutheran University into an entirely new kind of university, organized around themes instead of subjects. All departments would be dismantled and courses grouped around central ideas. The process was underway in the United States—and continues to this day. The chief problem that I could see was in staffing. I knew how to find suitable teachers for material studied in English Departments, and I had a good idea of the standard of knowledge and research that was expected of, say, a Shakespeare course. Also, I knew what level of expertise a student should reach by graduation, but we would have to build up the equivalent expectations for our teaching of themes.

Yet there was much to be said for the new approach. At a rather dull meeting of department chairmen, I drew up a list of theme programs that could be mounted at once, using courses that were already in existence. Knowing that I could count on an unusual tendency for co-operation among departments, I didn't see why we couldn't form committees to oversee the new programs, with a co-ordinator who would be the equivalent of a chairman of a conventional department.

The idea took off. Some of the possibilities we envisaged didn't work out, but many of the officially recognized interdepartmental programs we tried remain strong today.

The theme programs led to majors, also making courses available to students in other majors, and included: archaeology, Canadian studies, communication studies, film studies, fine arts, urban studies, and women's studies, with Third World studies added later. Not all were initiated at the beginning, the time of the threatened break-up of the department system, but they developed in answer to needs on campus. Thus we did not have to go out into the wide world to search for faculty—most were already here.

It is my impression that students like the flexibility of being able to choose interdepartmental majors as well as the conventional ones, or to choose optional courses from departments other than their primary ones.

The program for which students are willing to sleep in the corridors in order to be first in line for courses is communication studies, which has become the most popular arts major. We had been thinking about it for quite a long time before we ventured to present the program to a curriculum committee, and then year after year we saw it rejected because it was not conventional. We persisted, however, and finally launched a major attack, bringing in a schedule with most details covered, and with better arguments for such a program's introduction. The late Professor Glenn Carroll was the member of the committee who at that point inspired the rest of us, and his suggestions for the program were invaluable. At our final planning meeting he said, "What kind of program would we like to have had as undergraduates?" and we proceeded accordingly. I think we can give Glenn much of the credit for getting the whole thing finally past committees and into action.

By that time, practically every other university offered something similar. The idea had been around since McLuhan proclaimed, "The medium is the message." Along the way, the *Times Higher*

Education Supplement had called a conference near London, England, dealing with the planning of education in communication, which I was unable to attend, but I got in touch with someone at the Imperial College of Science and Technology who was interested, and with a former fellow student at the University of Toronto graduate school who was moving in the direction of media studies at McGill. They gave me moral support and advice. The problem was to open up English departments to new possibilities, while still ensuring that we gave more than adequate courses in Middle English literature and the rest. If we could develop and initiate a program that would give weight to the canon of English literature and still look at the social uses of language (and other media), we would prevent a "dumbing down" of higher education—or so we hoped. How could all this be done better than by departmental co-operation? The Psychology Department had experts in the study of how creatures exchanged information, and the Sociology, Political Science, History, and Philosophy departments could all contribute. Ultimately, we hoped to graduate students who, first, had something to communicate; second, had some knowledge of how various means of communication worked (film, photography, printing, etc.), and last, saw communication as a part of culture, to be studied like any other subject.

Once I was sure that the communication studies program was safely in place, I sent all my documents relating to the campaign to the archives, where they can be consulted. I would like to commend the English Department secretaries, first Susan Ramsay and then Charlotte Cox, who prepared the documents and were my right hands throughout. I find it interesting that Susan went on to get a degree in English and Charlotte to take courses in communication studies.

CHAPTER XIII

Governance of the English Department

On December 16, 1976, towards the end of my tenure, I heard that the academic vice-president told the dean he wanted less cordiality in the English Department and more insecurity; he wanted me to be a martinet who would enforce nine-to-five hours and make people publish. I had never taken the time to stand still and look at the department under my aegis and try to imagine what someone else thought of it. I looked ahead to the future, when problems would be solved, programs would be settled, and we would all relax. I didn't realize that the future I envisaged could be a rigid regime, stifling innovation and originality, and that the chaotic present could be viewed as a golden age.

I think my own measure for the state of the department was the success or failure of our graduates who generally did well. Even back in our time with Western, they rose to the top. In those days the University of Toronto had a notoriously difficult examination for entrance to its graduate courses for all but their own graduates, yet it held no terrors for our people. Pat Yantha recently reminded me that she passed it at the first try when others, including a now-famous academic personage failed.

I still get reminders of our success with students. A year or so ago I was greeted warmly on the street by an elderly gentleman who told me that he had been one of several young Germans who had come to us as students after completing high school in Germany. He told me he had since obtained a doctorate in German studies, and had taught at the University of Waterloo until offered an early retirement package. Now he was teaching English at a university in Koblenz, Germany. He said, "You didn't make any concessions, but you taught us to study." He assured me that he hadn't forgotten Shelley and Keats. And I hadn't forgotten *him* and his friends. They had been cleared for emigration by the occupying powers, I think. (One of them told me that he had been in Russia, but he was merely occupied in firing one of the big guns. I believed him.) They had received lectures on philosophy before leaving Germany. Denazification? For a time they tried to square everything I said with what they had heard in those lectures, but they soon became immersed in the literature itself, though I had to work a little harder to persuade them that it *was* literature, without the hallmarks of good German poetry or prose.

And one other example: recently I received a large envelope containing a photocopy of a short story that had just received the $10,000 first prize in the short story competition in a Toronto newspaper. The author, one of our honours English graduates, has been a civil servant for years, but she hadn't forgotten how to write. That was another thing we insisted on teaching them: how to observe human nature with a view to recreating it. We didn't do such a bad job after all, with our lack of insecurity and excess of cordiality.

I was perpetually on the lookout for faculty who could carry out the unspoken aims of the department. Remember that I am speaking of a time about forty years ago, when secondary-school English was not necessarily very exciting, and a student could move right through the undergraduate system to a doctorate thinking that an instructor's duty was to dictate lists of facts, good and bad aspects of a work, and character sketches in the study of fiction, so that they could be rehashed on an examination paper. In spite of the danger of inbreeding, I ended by offering our most promising graduates some financial help and a possibility of employment in summer schools as they moved towards doctorates. We took in graduates of other institutions in the same way. A few came through the testing process and have been among our best faculty. At that time only a few people had a doctorate in English, and they were being securely held by the institutions that produced them. We were then on the brink of a flood of students into universities, and everyone was trying to hire adequately trained instructors. We took to implementing a rigid schedule that went something like this: promising BAs were hired for absolutely no more than two years, and were given help in advancing their qualifications if their service had been satisfactory; promising MAs were hired for no more than three years, and would not be rehired without further study towards the doctorate.

We gave no reasons for not rehiring. Of course there were complications. We always had people going and coming, and we had to keep the way clear to bring back those who were meeting our requirements; I was never surprised when unsuspected weaknesses showed up in the long haul. One young scholar, for example, had a constitutional inability to mark examination papers. She fled the city and hid in Toronto, smoking pot in a back room until the examinations had been marked by someone else, and was quite affronted when she was not offered another contract.

We ended with a full complement of faculty with doctorates, except for a couple of members who had been held up by various mischances; they were retained, but as instructors. That decision had bothered my academic conscience, but necessary unfairness, and the accompanying guilt, seems to be a part of responsibility. When I retired, I had full confidence in the academic fitness of the whole department—and they *were* on their way to publication.

After much thought, I have decided not to try to write a history of the individuals in the English Department in my time, and not to write tributes to each of the members. That said, I would like to single out two professors who, more than I, made the department succeed: Jim Clark and Jane Campbell. Jim came first to Waterloo College. Professor Woodhouse had chosen the two of us to take Dr. Klinck's place. (There was an interregnum of a dear old chap who brought roses to the secretaries and had delightful chats with the students, and achieved not much else.) My friends at Western who marked all honours examination papers told me they were bowled over by the papers from the college that year—apparently not many texts had been studied—so Jim and I would have to pull things into shape and be unpopular for it. It was a hard year, but my colleague never wavered, and in time students accepted the new regime—especially as their marks improved. As I indicated earlier, Jim not only became our drama expert, and the head of Extension and summer school, but also served as Major Clark of the student reserves, COTC.

Jane Campbell came to the department later. I interviewed her in the old Round Room at Eaton's in Toronto. She, too, was a graduate student at the University of Toronto. (Did I mention that we were *all* still doctoral students in those days? We jokingly said we were ABTS: All But Thesis.) We completed the degrees in the summers while on leave from our faculty appointments. Jane, who had graduated from Queen's, came to us from Oxford where she had acquired a Bachelor of Literature, which was not considered quite enough for a tenured post in Canada. In due time she was awarded a doctorate from the University of Toronto and published "the book" that used to be regarded as enough for tenure. We were not yet lining up to get as many papers as possible into any available journal in order to hold our places in the hierarchy and to gain promotion. Both Jim and Jane proved to be trusted and respected by our students and the university community. If I were writing in the present tense only, I would say they were loved, but at that time we didn't use such words for professors. On a personal, non-academic level, I understood that at least three students had declared their intention of marrying the new female professor. I felt that was none of my business until one of them succeeded and became, as a spouse, an adjunct of the English Department. After making her reputation with studies of romanticism, Jane turned to feminist studies, and brought her common sense and wide knowledge to that new, challenging interdepartmental program, but she never forgot English literature in general.

I have made the above exceptions in pausing over individuals, not just because the two I have named were outstanding as teachers, but mostly because they came to be an unofficial part of the administration of the English Department. I had come in as appointed head, and though our university went through the democratizing change of electing chairmen, most of the former heads were autocrats to some degree. I proceeded to do what I thought best, but at any moment was not surprised if Jim or Jane came to me to say what the rest of the department thought, and I might make a *volte face*. Not long ago one of our retired members said to me, laughing, "Did you know that everyone else thought you had us scared stiff?" She was laughing because every member of the department had direct input into decisions, usually through Jim or Jane, and any suggestion could become part of departmental policy.

In time, we formed committees of students and others of faculty, with a third-level body linking both, but unofficially we went on much as before. I recall the problem regarding a trainee-faculty member who was just not satisfactory though he was very personable and extremely well-meaning. The student committee was inclined to make allowances, but his actual students submitted to me a petition citing his weaknesses and errors. I merely showed the petition to the student committee without any comment. As they read it, they started to shake their heads in pity, but also in agreement. When they handed it back, no one said anything, and they filed out sadly.

We were extremely fortunate to have had, for a time, that sort of understanding, but I was aware that it could turn stale and crush originality. At one point I had almost announced my intention to step down in favour of a department member with a background and personality very different from mine. I was sharing my deliberations with Jim, going over the good qualities of my potential successor, when he stopped me. I realized the department had talked the matter over and decided that the fluidity we lived with would be preferable to rigidity. As I have mentioned, the department used its unofficial constitution to oust my successor, the chairman, by standing up to the university administrators who had other ideas, which suggested that I would not have lasted long in my post had they wanted to depose *me*. I must sometime ask a political scientist how he would categorize the sort of government into which we had grown, which worked but looked to outsiders like the most blatant autocracy.

I have already mentioned a couple of our departmental secretaries who, perhaps more than I, ensured the Department of English at Waterloo Lutheran University "worked." If I had time, I should probably name *every* staff member of the old WLU: we were almost unbelievably fortunate in our employees. Some were Lutherans who felt a special pride in the new university, but many were not. All gave services far beyond the call of duty. I would like to single out four employees from the English Department: Barbara Foerster, Shirley Hinton, Susan Wright, and Charlotte Cox.

I do not recall how typing assistance was arranged in the very early days; I think there were two or three secretaries who helped whenever it was needed. But I do recall that Jim Clark sent out all his communications in his own longhand wherever possible. I was a fast and inaccurate typist myself, but could manage a letter. We used carbons for copies in those pre-photocopy days. Barbara Foerster was allotted to us when we were based in houses on Albert Street, and tactfully dealt with our comings and goings, keeping secrets that could have raised eyebrows if they had become public. I still regard her as a friend, but have never exchanged with her any gossip about colleagues long departed from our campus.

Shirley Hinton in her turn adopted each of us. After she and one of our members had departed to Vancouver, she kept in touch with us, and even went to nurse a former colleague when she caught the flu of the year. Shirley died of a stubborn virus not long after that.

Susan Wright had just arrived from England, and at her interview displayed a "swinging London" style, but, being a sharply intelligent and perceptive young woman, she came to her first day of work with pale lipstick and a sensible skirt. I used to be amused to see the respect academic visitors paid to the British girl at our front desk with her "good" accent. Finally, during her time, Charlotte Cox, who is typing part of this manuscript, became foster mother to the English Department and then an executive assistant in the office of the dean of Arts and Science.

Celebrating the twentieth year after my retirement, my friend Gerry Noonan (soon to be the late Gerry) arranged a little party at which he made a speech that referred to shifts in the relationship of faculty, staff, and administration over a long period of academic history.

Addressing me as *ex cathedra* (a little joke on the Lutheran establishment), he pointed out that, by retiring when I did, I had escaped such annoyances as, among other things, having to purchase a parking ticket at the university, having to waste time trying to decipher voice mail, and having to do my own typing thanks to the introduction of computers. Finally, he conceded that I no longer had to manage a department consisting of the likes of Gerry Noonan.

Dear Gerry! In his latter days, if I happened to be working late on this effort, he would take me home in his old green refurbished Mercedes-Benz. One evening as I was being transported, a passerby stopped, unbelieving, came over, and patted the front right fender appreciatively. The romance of man and machine!

The administration was not happy with our decision to forgo the MA in English until we had sufficient numbers of faculty and the time to do it properly. I could see how impolitic that approach was; one department, ruled by a professor who became president of the university, had jumped in very early to give graduate degrees. I had been required to attend some of those students' oral examinations, after having read the theses involved, and in most instances was not sure that I was listening to better performances than ones I expected from our honours students in a seminar. I should add that by that time the MA had become devalued almost everywhere, partly because the unprecedented rise in enrolments found English departments understaffed and without the time to spend on MA candidates to ensure that they would attain another level of erudition. I was not depending on my own impressions of the decline in quality. The matter was discussed in scholarly circles and there were many in favour of maintaining standards. But the liberating of the culture, which reached the universities in the late sixties and early seventies, made the way harder. In time the movement may have made it easier for our English Department to offer an MA, though teaching loads were not greatly diminished and I felt that the demands for frequent publishing of scholarly articles and books were increased.

The co-operation between departments, which I have empha-
sized, made it possible to remind students that other disciplines
could give new insights into works of literature. We were fortunate, too, in being in an environment that took for granted the idea
that learning and the arts were not confined to specialists. In my
early years at Waterloo College, a strong influence on campus was
that of Mrs. Aksim, who became house mother in the girls' residence. She had the residents talking about literature as a part of
everyday socializing. Thus, though we worked in the middle of an
anti-intellectual culture that prized financial success beyond scholarly achievements, our students could see other points of view, and
their lives were thereby much enriched.

More recently, I keep referring back to a review by A.N. Wilson
of a book by Harold Bloom, *The Western Canon* (*Spectator*, February 4, 1995). I quote just two paragraphs written by Bloom:

> In the last quarter century, the arts faculties of western universities
> have been taken over by opinionated idealogues who deny any of the
> canons of taste which informed and illumined previous generations.
> Books became "texts" to be fooled about with but not to be ab-
> sorbed into the inner self. The concept of The Canon was aban-
> doned altogether; and great writers who had been the shared interior
> experience of the civilized world were either not read at all—how
> many people under the age of 30 today have read *The Iliad* or *Par-
> adise Lost?*—or denounced from the posture of some half-baked ide-
> ology, feminist, leftist or otherwise. Adolescents scarcely out of
> short trousers were encouraged to pass judgment on Jane Austen
> for her supposed unsoundness on the slave trade but it is doubtful
> whether they ever read her books.
>
> Precisely why students of literature have become amateur po-
> litical scientists, uninformed sociologists, incompetent anthropol-
> ogists, mediocre philosophers, and over determined cultural histo-
> rians, while a puzzling matter, is not beyond all conjecture.

The above refers to the extreme of too much breadth in an English
program. A later article on Oxford (*Spectator*, February 12, 2000)
describes the lax state of affairs that can come into being or, rather,
sneak up on a community that has not looked at itself critically
for some time. At Waterloo Lutheran University we tried to steer

between both extremes. Perhaps, as the Oxford rebels say, "The best judge of a teacher is the pupil," and I should leave it at that.

I am trying to keep my resolution to write about the faculty of our English Department only in general terms to avoid any imbalance, but I am not sure that I will be successful in my resolve. I must say that I cannot imagine another department that could have such diversity of creative individuals and such loyalty to one another as a community. In this connection I wish to mention the late John Chamberlin. When they knew his time was limited, the department called a special meeting, and each member told what John meant to him or her—a eulogy before the fact. One of them pointed out that the event proved the value of their discipline: language is invaluable to human beings. At the time Gerry did not tell them that he too had received his summons from above and was saying good-bye inwardly to colleagues and friends.

Before I leave the discussion of the English Department at Waterloo Lutheran University, I want to repeat what I have hinted at before: we owed much of our success to the co-operation and help of the rest of the university, which has been going on for a long time. I append a copy of an article describing a production of *The Indian Queen* by our Faculty of Music, from *Laurier News*, June 20, 2000.

Faculty of Music, Theatre Laurier joining forces
in production of the *Indian Queen*

It's got wonderful music and a fanciful plot; Baroque dance and swordfights and special effects.

And, says Michael Purves-Smith of Laurier's Music Faculty, when local theatre-lovers gather in the Theatre Auditorium for the Wilfrid Laurier University production of the *Indian Queen*, they're in for a "spectacular" evening of entertainment quite unlike anything ever before staged at Laurier, in Canada, and quite possibly, in North America.

"Our approach has been to make this as much of a spectacle as it would have been in the late 17th century," says Purves-Smith, who is co-staging the production with Adam Qualter, Director of Theatre Laurier. "There's so much happening in this production, I can't imagine that anyone coming to it wouldn't be fascinated. It's a very unusual theatrical experience."

With music by Henry and Daniel Purcell and text by John Dry-den and Robert, Earl of Howard, the *Indian Queen* is an English semi-opera that dates back to 1795. It is a true restoration tragedy, and like many plays of its era is set in the British Indies. The *Indian Queen* offers a complex and somewhat farfetched story of melo-drama and stage magic, and showcases some of the most beautiful and characteristic music of Henry Purcell, who was the foremost composer of his time. The *Indian Queen* was Purcell's last work, completed after Purcell's death by his brother, Daniel.

The Laurier production, says Purves-Smith, may well be the first time in North America that the *Indian Queen* has been per-formed as a semi-opera—with full text as Purcell would have expe-rienced it 300 years ago. Unlike an opera, where the music is contin-uous, and the musical, where the music is interwoven with the drama, in a semi-opera the actions are divided between spoken dia-logue and elaborate musical interludes that are only loosely related to the story line.

The *Indian Queen* is a first for Laurier in several other ways. It will be the first major production presented jointly by the Faculty of Music and Theatre Laurier. It will also be the first time that a pro-duction of this size has been performed entirely by Laurier stu-dents—in the dance roles, the singing roles, and the acting roles. In total, more than 90 students will take part in the production.

"It's a bit like a giant jigsaw puzzle. We need a Baroque orches-tra. Then there's the acting cast; then the dancers, some of whom come from the acting cast, others the musical; then the singing cast. We're collaborating with the Chapel Choir because we need a choir. And we had to bring in a fight master to help stage a fight scene and a Baroque dance specialist to help with the historic dances," says Purves-Smith.

The Faculty of Music and Theatre Laurier presents the *Indian Queen* on Friday, January 28 and Saturday, January 29 at 8 p.m. in the Theatre Auditorium. Tickets, $15 for adults, $10 for seniors, and $7 for students, are available at the door.

The producer told me that he gave credit to the English Depart-ment for providing actors and other assistants. I later pointed out to him that he had helped me as well as our students to understand an art form that today, in itself—studied only as words on a page—has little effect. The combining of the correct movements, gestures, and costumes, as well as staging, speaking, and singing, showed me why the Stuart theatres were full (as I am sure they were).

Back in the early years of Waterloo Lutheran University, we celebrated a Shakespearean anniversary by inviting Professor Knox of University College, University of Toronto, to address us. Our music department provided a madrigal choir, properly costumed, who sat around a table and sang as those in Tudor and early Stuart society might have done in their domestic setting. (I seem to recall candles in hands as the choir filed down the auditorium steps to the stage. What would the fire authorities say today?) Professor Knox, who had been a popular professor of many of us as graduate students, enjoyed the ceremony as much as we could have wished.

I have already mentioned the surprise W.H. Auden showed when our music department provided a first-rate soloist to perform an aria for which he had written the libretto. In other words, our various departments did not mind helping each other look better in the eyes of the public. Have I said we were lucky?

CHAPTER XIV

Student Unrest

⎯⎯⎯⎯⎯ ↬ ⎯⎯⎯⎯⎯

IN THIS RECALLING OF WATERLOO LUTHERAN UNIVERSITY in the years from 1960 to 1973, I have mentioned some of the effects on our university of what might be termed unrest—unrest among students and also in the ranks of the faculty. Looking back at that time from the perspective of new labour and global capitalism, along with the computer revolution, the general leftism of the 1960s seems almost naive. Tremendous forces were in contention all around us, but students and faculty alike felt that they could play effective parts in influencing events, though even now we are just beginning to understand the political and economic pressures that provided the energy for those forces.

A few reminders of crises in those years will provide examples. The defeat of fascism did not bring peace in 1945. It only brought the challenge of Stalinism to the West. For many academics the Soviet system had seemed to promise a brave new world. In my previous book I mentioned one of our professors of the 1950s who told his students so, and talked expansively about his visit to Russia and his impressions of a system that had brought happiness as well as economic justice to all. Recent revelations from Soviet files have shown that at that time academics and opinion moulders in the West were being cultivated and sometimes rewarded for their championing of Stalinism. For myself, acquaintance with a Ukrainian refugee who had lived through the Five Year Plan only because her mother had been especially ingenious at hiding food from the government inspectors, along with a certain amount of my own reading, had made me a bit skeptical about the Russian paradise.

In addition, that time of Mao and the Cultural Revolution was also favoured by left-inclining gurus of Canadian opinion. I tried to retain an open mind about China: as a charm against campus activists I had bought in London a copy of the Little Red Book, and if anyone—student or colleague—came to my office to proselytize, I would take it down from the shelf and read a bit aloud. I recall most of it as being quite innocuous.

For universities in the US the foremost challenge was that of the Vietnam War. We had watched it grow from early disagreements to a division between right and left (South and North Vietnam) with steady absorption of outside forces that had gone to help one group or the other. I suppose I should not blame many of our local protestors against this "War" for not knowing much about it, because I myself didn't know much more. I recall that in a literature class one day a student unexpectedly asked, "What do *you* think of Vietnam?" Without stopping to consider, I replied with my basic belief: "They should never have let the French back in." That provoked an immediate retort from a student who gathered that I was a simple racist, and asked, "What have you got against the French?"

I realized that for this student, at least, the problems in Quebec were getting mixed up with the problems of the ending of colonialism in Southeast Asia, but I didn't feel that it was an English professor's job to sort out the two, and went back to my lecture in English literature.

Then there was the influence of political events in Cuba. Batista had fled in 1959, taking the good will of American capitalism with him and leaving a space for the friends of communism. The final break in diplomatic relations with the US in 1961 and the missile crisis of the next year made Cuba an enemy of the right, and thus a sort of protégé of the left. I do not recall much discussion of Cuba on our campus, but there were signs of admiration for "Che" Guevara. From my own memory I can draw the picture of an exile I met in Italy who was marking time until Castro would be overthrown and his firm could return to its rewarding investments in the Cuban economy. I never asked what his business interests were, but I am quite sure they were not anti-social; there had been some, especially attractive to high-spending visitors, that were less admirable. My sympathies were with Castro, but I was never called upon to demonstrate them.

If one were sensitive to trends in the US, the movement led by Martin Luther King, Jr. might have aroused one's sympathy, but I do not recall any spillover on our campus from all the actions of his forces. At that time, apart from a few students from Africa and elsewhere, ours was predominantly a "white" institution.

To the south of us, student activism rose steadily during the 1960s to climax in strikes on at least two hundred campuses in 1970. Groups such as Students for a Democratic Society had outposts in Canada, and the natural identification with other young people against obvious injustices had an effect on activism, partly in response to a general demand for equal civil rights—and partly as a result of the migration to Canada of young people avoiding the draft for the Vietnam War. These academic refugees arrived at a time when the great "rise" in student enrolment in Canada coincided with a great dip in the number of qualified faculty available, and so they became part of the Canadian university culture, some of them as faculty, bringing their views on civil liberties and national rights with them.

I have sketched some of the currents which were in the air in the period we think of as the sixties and that made for student unrest, but was there anything more specific—anything amiss in the universities themselves that could have inflamed resentment even without external prompting? Two key words of the time were *democracy* and *relevance*. The government of universities in general was denounced as oligarchic (a term used by one of our faculty rebels) and the cry was for participation. Relevance meant, I think, discussion by the students—in any course—of causes in which they were interested. That would involve a rubbishing of the syllabus and of examinations. Would evaluation and final marks, if any, depend then on "right thinking"? At least one American university had no grading of students.

Personally I was aware that much could be changed for the better on our campus, but I felt that by steady and persistent work we could evolve into a more effective body, and I did not have much sympathy with the belief that admitting students to university deliberations on the same level as faculty and administrators would result in communal harmony regarding curriculum, instruction, evaluation, and management.

I had noticed that many of the protestors were young men who sought out the company of male members of faculty. I had learned that they were sons of men who had been in the armed forces and, on discharge, had started a family, or a business, or a career in some profession, and had little time to bond with their children. One such young man on our campus insisted on eating in the faculty dining room, remaining to chat with any professor who was available and willing. The faculty members tended to resent this and the atmosphere was not exactly that of a happy family. The same student acted out being an example of deprivation, going so far as to eat out of garbage cans, thus showing solidarity with the poor and rejected.

A few faculty members seemed to enjoy sitting on the floor in a circle with students. I am not aware of the subject of their conversations—perhaps their feelings? I am sure no harm was done, and it may have been helpful to all of them.

Waterloo Lutheran University certainly seemed more peaceful in the 1960s than some other places, except for bomb threats that tended to be made by phone when a term test was coming. We did have a day of protest in which students roamed through the arts building in procession, shouting and holding one another up. The attractively disheveled look of one of the girls aroused my suspicions, and a rumour that the juice and cookies provided by a student committee may have included ingredients unknown to Betty Crocker rather confirmed my impression that in order to get a show of protest from our student body, the organizers had had to resort to more than the usual incentives.

"I would have been worried if we hadn't had Bill Ballard." These words were elicited by a recent mention of the student unrest of the late 1960s to someone who had been here at the time. Bill Ballard was the student president that year, in some ways an ordinary geography major, but in others a man of the world who probably knew more about commercial and political human nature than our administrators. His father was a major shareholder in Maple Leaf Gardens, and in the Maple Leafs, the hockey team of the moment. Thus he was close to professional sport, which may have been a little less venal in those days. Bill knew the world ran on wheeling and dealing, and not on vague if fashionable enthusiasms.

At some point, department chairmen were bidden, two or three at a time, to meet with a student committee that would point out our errors and weaknesses and interrogate us in general. It looked to me as if they mostly wanted to see authority on the "hot seat." Were they getting even with their too-busy fathers who had substituted cold instructions for warm interaction?

When it was my turn to meet, I shared the onslaught with the head of one of the science departments, and forgot my own discomfort in my concern for his blood pressure. His face got redder and redder as he struggled to control his indignation at being treated so disrespectfully by young whippersnappers. (In fact, some time later he did have a stroke that left him considerably less able.) The only relief was that our student president acted as a moderator, and after the meeting, in answer to my inquiry of what we should do in reply said, "The English Department and the Geography Department have nothing to worry about."

In all, we really got off lightly in English. I have forgotten if we ever did have any formal student complaints. Since the department was organized to have student input through the proper committees, and since all departmental papers were deposited in the archives, a researcher will be able to check there for any evidence that may have escaped my memory. A student I know who was involved in interrogating and haranguing other departments told me that some such meetings were very bitter.

My own feeling about the relations between various areas of the university was that we were a very late example of the guild system. University titles still reflect that system: bachelor (having passed the first stage of tutelage), master (a workman qualified to teach apprentices), and doctor (a learned or authoritative teacher). The word apprentice is, for me, the key. The student is moving along a gradient that will in time make him the equal of anyone who has attained the same level in the craft. Only other craft workers can assess his worthiness to advance, and until he is a good barrel maker, for example, I am not ready to receive his input on barrel staves. I know this is not democracy, but it is a system that still works. Along the same lines, the beginning piano student is not invited to instruct his teacher in the techniques he is just starting to acquire.

We had many campus problems worse than the above and would probably have solved them quietly had it not been for the events in the great nation to the south and the subsequent influx of refugees who brought their trouble to Canadian academics.

At the beginning of our most disrupted academic year, at our initial meeting of students and faculty, new professors were introduced, welcomed, and invited to respond. One who had just arrived from the US replied with an excited attack on government, higher education, and all their works. Bill Ballard, who was the chairman of the meeting, rose after the peroration and merely said, "Professor X, welcome to Canada." The applause expressed something like a sense of relief. After all, Canada was not the United States, and Canadians were less incendiary than their neighbours.

CHAPTER XV

Faculty Unrest

H AS THERE BEEN A THOROUGH, unbiased, professional study of
faculty unrest in Canadian universities in the lifetime of
Waterloo Lutheran University, or going back a bit in the post-war
years? During my own experience, which dates from the late 1930s
at the University of Saskatchewan to the University of Toronto,
and later to Waterloo College and the University of Western Ontario
of which we were a part, I did not encounter any faculty subversion
that I remember. There were conditions that faculty unions of today
would deplore, especially the buddy system, or more politely, nepo-
tism, if one could include in those terms favours to colleagues,
friends, and benefactors. Those favours could include bursaries and
appointments, and there was no effective mechanism for protest or
redress.

There were faculty associations on individual campuses, and
the Canadian Association of University Teachers, which was becoming more confident, and perhaps more ready for confrontation.
At faculty conferences, as time went on, I noticed a greater sensitiv-
ity to threats against freedom of opinion and speech. We had our own
problems at Waterloo Lutheran University as I have shown, but
handled them within the campus. Those who were most alert to the
possibility of imposition of controls on expressions of openness in
Canada were not all young rebels, but often men of experience.
They could have been described as leftist, and they may have voted

CCF (for the uninitiated, a party with religious beginnings that hoped to rule through democratic co-operation as the Co-operative Commonwealth Federation).

The outbreak came in 1958 at United College, an institute under the United Church, a body that had been formed as part of the University of Manitoba when a large part of the Presbyterian and Methodist congregations of Canada joined as one. Both parent bodies had educated several generations of Manitobans, and United College inherited their reputation for excellence. To the outside viewer, there appeared to be no repression there; surely in other places the administrators ruled with a heavier hand, but ironically, revolution tends to occur in less oppressive situations, as it did there.

Known as the Crowe, it entertained readers of newspapers and listeners of radio for some time and may deserve another mention. One day, the head of United found on his desk a personal letter from one faculty member to another, denouncing the college and its administrators. The attached note read, "How is this for loyalty?" or something to that effect. The unfortunate head must have wished later than he had thrown it into the waste basket—or, even better, shredded it. Instead he felt that he had to discipline the sender. The newspaper files of the time will give you the whole story. The Canadian Association of University Teachers (CAUT) was brought in and United was condemned. (That was, of course, before Trudeau's Bill of Rights, but there were plenty of reasons for objecting to the misuse of a private communication on the part of the United College administration.)

But was this really a private communication? A friend of mine assured me that he had been shown a copy of the letter. Was it a plant? Was there a plot to trap the head? If so, why? United College has since become the University of Winnipeg; it was a challenge (for funds) to the provincial university. United was too much of a denominational college.

Perhaps only the paranoid would go further, but I was reminded of another crisis that we all studied in Canadian history as the Manitoba Schools Question of 1890. The nineteenth-century contro-

versy involved Protestants objecting to government funding for
Roman Catholic schools. Some contributors to the debate objected
to funding for any schools involved with a religious denomination.
(Mennonites, too, were ready to claim funding for their Manitoba
schools.)

Had that dispute, which was carried east and which figured in
federal elections, left a general suspicion of *all* educational institutions with religious attachments? Far-fetched the idea may be, but
I have wondered if the decision of the Ontario government to ap-
prove the founding of the University of Waterloo, at the expense of
Waterloo College which was in all but name an operating university,
was a carry-over from the bitter split in the Ontario Conservative
party in the previous century. I suggest that a future researcher try
to find out if in 1959–60 there was anything left of the prejudice
that in 1890 inspired remarks like the following editorial: "We
shall not allow the state to support religion, we shall not allow the
church to control the state, we shall not return to the civilization of
the dark ages" (Lovell Clark, "The Manitoba School Question,"
Winnipeg Tribune, March 27, 1895). That was Manitoba, of course.
And Ontario? L.C. Clark declares, "The militant Protestantism
and Anglo-Saxon socialism, to which the Conservative Party [in
Ontario] succumbed in the eighteen-nineties remained to plague it
long after-ward" (Canadian Historical Association, *Annual Report*,
1961). Could one symptom of that plague have been the pressure
against Lutheran Waterloo College—and against Roman Catholic
colleges—instituted by the Ontario Conservatives in the late 1950s?

But what has that to do with unrest on campuses in the 1960s?
In the 1890s one objection to aid for church-related schools was
that they would be restrictive, stifling free thought and speech. In
the 1950s the move against church-related colleges may have involved the fear that they would be against a relaxation of social
codes, against scientific advancement and theory, especially Dar-
winism, and against what we could subsume under the term leftist
ideas in economics and politics. I have a feeling that the unrest,
even in large state universities in the 1960s, may have had the same
excuse, especially where there may have been some reminders of

their heredity—so many of our higher educators had come from ecclesiastical origins. Faculty rebels in the 1960s may in part have been rebels against the non-conformist conscience as represented by ministers and parents. They took the position against all institutions of higher education that their forefathers had taken against Catholics in the Manitoba Schools Question.

There is one more reason for a distrust of universities in Ontario—a reluctance to test the attitude of the general voter to the granting of public funds to institutions presumed to be for an "elite." That hesitation was evident as long ago as 1901 when the University of Toronto was asking for a new building, and it may still apply more than one hundred years later.

So the social and political challenges of the 1960s were bubbling up on campuses all over the world, and it was not surprising that the intensity rose in a small university in southern Ontario. Instead of trying to recall all the eruptions at Waterloo Lutheran University, I will mention one that drew together a number of concerns from far and near, and that finally developed into an argument about civil rights: the celebrated George Haggar case, celebrated, that is, by the press. For my information I am drawing on a file of clippings, dated from 1966 to 1968, which I hope will some day be donated to the WLU archives, supplementing the file with my own recollections.

I advise a researcher that the Haggar case, rather than written as a mundane essay, would be better treated as a novel with a sympathetic hero of exotic origin. It would include a trace of the romantic, as well as a modicum of some of the questions, global and personal, that excited the late 1960s. My first hint to the novelist would be not to begin by refreshing his memory of that time, but to read the Bible, particularly the book of Genesis, chapters sixteen and twenty-five, noting that minus one "g" the name of our hero is that of Hagar, the mother of Ishmael. Of Ishmael it was said, "And he will be a wild man; his hand will be against every man, and every man's hand against him." Hagar, you recall, fled into the wilderness with her son.

George Haggar was Lebanese. I know nothing about his early years, but if, as I surmise, they were passed in Lebanon, he would have lived through the French mandate, the British invasion in

1941, and the strife surrounding on the creation of a Jewish homeland. Now he was an exile, a twentieth-century Ishmael.

If his surname reminds the fanciful of an ancient separation of peoples, his first name George suggests a somewhat later separation—that between early Christians and their neighbours. St. George is said to have died for his faith in 225 AD. The crusaders made pilgrimages to his shrine seven hundred years later. In fact, Pope John Paul II asked for pardon for that incursion of European Christians that further destabilized the already riven Middle East. Symbolically our George's background was not a peaceful or stable one.

At the first faculty gathering, at the beginning of George's second year with us, the university president cordially asked a few faculty members to address us on the subject, recalled facetiously from schooldays, "What I Did in My Summer Holidays." After some pleasant and harmless accounts, George was called upon. He got up and said, "I was in the Six Days' War." He went on to lambaste Israel and Zionists and all the enemies of Arabs, to our great surprise, because we had no idea of his passionate support of the Syrians, Jordanians, and Egyptians in their disputes with Israel. After the meeting I saw a solid-looking faculty member approach him, saying something like this: "George, I should tell you that I am collecting money for a committee for the defence of Israel." Thus the Arab–Israeli confrontation made its appearance on our campus.

But that was not the first dispute George had been involved in. I have no access to his CV, so cannot say anything about his life before coming to Waterloo Lutheran University, but the file of newspaper clippings contains some references to his earlier career. Before November 1966, his publications included papers on Algeria, on the Kurds, and on the role of the US in the creation of Israel.

Another reference in a Toronto newspaper states the following: "Haggar was fired last May from Southern University in New Orleans when he joined students in a 19-day strike during which Louisiana Governor John McKeithan was captured and held to win student demands" (September 1968).

The Vietnam War continued to be one of his preoccupations. Sometime in 1967–68 he had had a dispute at a meeting on campus with Paul Martin, Sr., who represented the Canadian government.

George asked him from the floor if Canada would give aid to Ho Chi Minh in the form of medicines and food for the suffering. Paul Martin, Sr. replied, in effect, that the Canadian government would look favourably on such a prospect, but he doubted that George could get permission for the donation because one could not get through to the communist leader. George shouted, "I can!" and rushed from the meeting to a telephone in his office. There he spent a long time trying different connections but all in vain. Later in the faculty room he told me, with a glint of humour, that he could have got through at once via Moscow, but did not want to. He was in effect telling me that he had a special relationship with Moscow, a revelation that did not surprise me. No, I did not call the RCMP. In crossing borders, it is likely that George had at some time sworn that he was not, nor had ever been, a member of the Communist Party, and doubts about that statement could have been embarrassing. I did not think the safety of the nation was involved and I kept my information to myself. Also, George tended to fight in the open—I thought—and was not particularly effective because his mode of attack was based on argument and polemic, not on dirty tricks, and, I was pretty sure, not at all on terrorism. What he would think, or thinks now about the recent revelations about Western involvement in Arab terrorism back in the 1960s I cannot imagine.

So far his hand was not against every man, but when his contract was not renewed, he saw enemies closer to home. Our file of newspaper cuttings shows that by January of 1968, "a major storm [was] brewing over the dismissal by Waterloo Lutheran University of a professor who has constantly supported the Arab cause in the Middle East and opposed US involvement in Vietnam." He filed an appeal to the CAUT, citing a violation of his right to academic freedom, but the CAUT was helpless in face of the contract that Professor Haggar had signed. In the first place, it was a contract with no provision for renewal, and there was no requirement that reasons be given for tenure being terminated. The CAUT *did* assert that a section in the contract that required that disparagement of Christianity and of the Lutheran Church in particular "is to be made in a constructive manner for the welfare of Christianity rather than its detriment," which was "decidedly unacceptable." In addition, the procedures for dealing with appointment, promotion, tenure, and so on were "unacceptably authoritarian," and the plaintiff should have been given a statement in writing regarding the non-renewal of the contract. The Trudeau declaration of rights in 1982 might have given a basis for a more drastic reaction, but that was 1968, and after the CAUT decision Professor Haggar had no other court than public opinion. The student council was sympathetic to him, and the newspapers were at least ready to give his cause an airing, but there was no great surge of support.

The WLU faculty were living very close to the situation, and, as I recall, their reaction was "poor George." After he had made a last impassioned plea to a faculty group, he retired to his office and, with his head sunk in his hands on his desk, he sat there all night. He might have felt even worse if he had known that the campus security officer, a competent, brotherly type, kept an eye on him off and on during the night—the outside fire escape was a perfect base for observation. He was afraid of a suicide attempt, the guard said. George never confided his feelings to any of us. Many students were on his side, and a rumour of a romantic attraction to a young woman in the French Department was circulating, but I know nothing of other supporters, such as family and friends. I *have* been told recently that three faculty members made a formal visit to his office to beg him to resign because of the negative publicity he was generating towards the university, but nothing of that was known at that time.

That publicity was several fronts. In November 1967 he ran for a seat on Waterloo City Council, promising, if elected, to address such problems as land speculation in the city and the oligarchic running of Waterloo Lutheran University. "What infuriates me most," he said, "is the predominance of utilitarians within the universities, who instead of cultivating minds, produce robots to make the world safe for capitalism" (*Cord Weekly*, November 24, 1967). He did not become an alderman.

The complaint regarding non-renewal of his contract was shifted from the question of academic rights and free expression to an accusation of racial discrimination—a Jewish member of faculty wrote very courageously to the *Record* to state that she had never felt the slightest discrimination at Waterloo Lutheran University, giving Dr. Haggar an excuse to write an answer, misinterpreting her letter and attacking the university further for having few PhDs on the faculty and a poor record of publication.

The battle widened when he started applying for posts in other universities. He declared that he had been turned down by five Ontario institutions when he applied for vacant positions on their faculties. He claimed that he was refused because he was an Arab, "and that he [had] been a spokesman for Canadian Arabs in their opposition to the State of Israel" (*Toronto Daily Star*, September 16, 1969). Our clipping file includes rebuttals from York and what must have been an almost final article citing a letter from the principal of King's College, stating that it would be "impossible to hire somebody in the faculty ... who would be openly hostile to the state of Israel." That was because the university was "negotiating with the Canadian Jewish community for establishment of a centre for Jewish students at the university." The same article states: "Professor George Haggar said last night that he will have to leave Canada within three weeks—though it's the last thing he wants to do." Presumably his permission to stay in the country was running out. As far as I know, that was our last news of the exile.

I would like to return to the novelist who might be tempted to use the Haggar story as historical fiction, a genre that seems to be getting closer to academic respectability today. My first reaction as I stopped to review my prosaic account was pity for the waste of human potential—potential for a good and fulfilled life, as well as for a contribution to the well-being of others, especially that of students who responded to the intellectual challenge, more so when it was against repression of all kinds. At Waterloo Lutheran University we saw one example of the effect on a gifted individual of a political division that had its roots a very long time ago.

CHAPTER XVI

The Ending

W ATERLOO LUTHERAN UNIVERSITY ENDED IN 1973. It had lasted
since 1960, but lasted is hardly the word for that time of building an institution that later became known as Wilfrid Laurier University, an institution that is more than holding its own in the
Maclean's ratings and which, in spite of the provincial crisis in
funding, is desperately planning to educate the hundreds of new
applicants who want to come to a small place with a good reputation. The Lutherans had held on as long as possible, but with a similar monetary crisis, they had to accept provincial status for their
university. A few devoted supporters, led by a couple of faculty
members, tried to find other sources of income. With much regret,
I wasn't one of them.

Was it worthwhile, that holding of the redoubt for over a dozen
years? It cost a lot in terms of overwork and anxiety. It involved
everyone from cleaners to administration, and it was held against
odds such as religious prejudice. As a newcomer to this part of
southern Ontario, and as a prairie latitudinarian, I regarded Lutheranism as being on the same level as other mainstream religions.
But I became aware that there were citizens and taxpayers who, on
religious grounds, would not support Waterloo Lutheran University.

In Lutheran congregations themselves, many had wanted Waterloo College to join the University of Waterloo in 1959–60; they had
been outvoted at a special meeting where the decision was made to

go it alone. They were not especially anxious to see us succeed, nor were certain friends of the faculty members who had threatened to move as a body to the University of Waterloo, and had been unable to force Waterloo College to move with them. Almost all were left without jobs for a time as the new university refused to hire most of them, and they were perhaps reluctant or ashamed to come back to the college.

Even now I can only guess at the motives of the Ontario government, but at the time it looked as though it was determined to create a new public university, and to allow local church-related colleges to exist only on its campus, under its supervision, financially as well as academically. At first, after our decision to remain on our own, we felt no overt sign of disapproval, but in time we could see that the government would not give us adequate funding. They *did* leave us on our own as a public institution, and that may have been because they could not ignore the ingenuity and dedication behind our success. (Also, the son of a very prominent politician was one of our students.)

University funding has long been a sensitive issue in Ontario politics. Back in 1901 Premier Ross had to deal with lobbying by alumni of the University of Toronto who were asking for "general support and a new building." An article on the subject in the Spring 2000 volume of the University of Toronto magazine continues, "Premier Ross ... was worried about the political consequences of giving too much support to what many considered an elite group. 'I think that the university question is the most dangerous one we have taken up this session,' he wrote to a cabinet colleague in 1901. 'Although our followers will stand by us, I am quite uneasy as to the effect upon the country'" (p. 35).

In an article celebrating an anniversary of University College of the University of Toronto, we find a reminder of the infighting of those days between church-related academic institutions and secular ones.

> When the new University College building opened for classes in 1859, the Toronto *Leader* called it "the hope of the nation." But it was quite a fight to get that far.

UC was founded in 1853 to be the teaching body of the newly re-
structured University of Toronto. Opening with 113 students in the
former Parliament of Upper Canada building on Front Street, UC
moved three times in seven years.

   With rival, church-affiliated colleges plotting to grab UC's funding, officials decided to invest their endowment in one big building.
As Ontario Politician John A. Macdonald (later Canada's first prime
minister) advised, "even Methodists couldn't steal bricks and mor-
tar."

The government did pay for a new physics building: that was
the way history was moving, and later the government gave more
aid to the University of Toronto, but in 1973 Waterloo Lutheran
University had a special disadvantage. It was the last remaining
private institution of higher learning—and one run by a religious
minority. That may be why it had to metamorphose into a provincial institution, though (irony of ironies) named after a great Liberal,
not an Ontario Conservative.

"Plus ça change" they say, *"plus c'est la même chose."* Would
Wilfrid Laurier University today be high in the *Maclean's* ranking of
universities, and first in a government survey reported in the *Globe
and Mail* of March 20, 2000, had it not derived from an original
that both prized scholarship and cultivated a realistic awareness of
life. I have before me a page from *Laurier News* of May 27, 1997, fea-
turing five of the most distinguished graduates that year. One of
them was hired by a US company as a "business and information
technology analyst." The training that impressed his new employ-
ers was an updated version of the old business program. To my initial surprise when I read the account, the other four graduates have
religious affiliations. The top student of the year says she "owes
her accomplishments to a supportive family and commitment to her
faith." She adds that she arranged her academic work so that she
could "participate in family and church life." After her honeymoon—
and convocation—she was to teach in a private Christian school.
The winner of the Bronze Medal went on to be "an international
intern with the Mennonite Economic Development Association"
in Nicaragua. The Gold Medallist in social work is teaching at Reni-

son College, a church-related college of the University of Waterloo. The last, awarded the Alumni Gold Medal for Music, is "both Music Director and Youth Director at Redeemer Lutheran Church in Waterloo, helping as well with pastoral care. She ... teaches vacation Bible school and conducts Bible studies for young adults." One would think that Wilfrid Laurier University of 1997 was still Waterloo Lutheran University.

I realize that I haven't mentioned the status of Waterloo Lutheran Seminary. It is still a discreet presence on the campus, a little removed from the other buildings, but with the same open way to its front door, and to the chapel housing the Casavant organ, which belongs to the Faculty of Music, and was recently used by them for a celebration of the 250th anniversary of the death of J.S. Bach. Students and friends are welcome to services in the chapel, and it enters their lives in other ways. Recently I was at a funeral of a former graduate of Waterloo Lutheran University. It was held in a United Church, but sharing the pulpit and giving the sermon was a former head of the seminary who said he had married the deceased and her husband, a fellow student, and baptized their children. It occurred to me then that when the Lutherans gave over the university to the government of Ontario, they did not give up their presence. The value of that presence I must leave you to decide, but in these days of pervasive distrust and self-seeking, the most rigorous opponents of religion in education might be persuaded to acknowledge the seminary's considerable accomplishment.

Appendix

*Presidents of Waterloo College, Waterloo Lutheran University,
Wilfrid Laurier University*

1914–1918	Rev. Preston Laury
1918–1920	Rev. Carroll H. Little
1920–1925	Rev. Emil Hoffmann (died April 11, 1926) (Resigned as president September 1925)
1926–1927	Rev. A.A. Zinck
1927–1928	Dean Alexander O. Potter
1928–1931	Dean Froats
1931–1942	Rev. Fredrick Clausen (died August 5, 1942)
1942–1944	No president
1944–1954	Rev. Helmut Lehmann
1954–1959	Gerald Hagey
1959–1961	H.M. Axford
1961–1967	Dr. W.J. Villaume (became president in July but installed in October)
1967–1968	Dr. Henry Endress (acting)
1968–1978	Dr. Frank Peters
1978–1982	Dr. Neale Taylor
1982–1992	Dr. John Weir
1992–1997	Dr. Lorna Marsden
Sept. 1997–present	Dr. Robert G. Rosehart

Presidents and Executive Heads
of the Seminary

1911–1914   Prof. Ottomar Lincke (acting president)
1914–1918   Dr. Preston Laury (president)
1918–1920   Rev. Carroll H. Little (acting president)
1920–1926   Rev. Emil Hoffmann (president, resigned September 1925)
1926–1927   Rev. A.A. Zinck

Chancellors, 1961 to present,
Waterloo Lutheran University/
Wilfrid Laurier University

May 20, 1961–July 1961   The Hon. W.D. William Daum Euler
Dec. 6, 1964–June 1972   The Hon. W. Ross Macdonald
June 1972–Apr. 30, 1977   The Hon. Paul Joseph Martin
July 4, 1977–July 3, 1985   The Hon. John Black Aird
May 25, 1986–May 29, 1990   Maureen Forrester
July 12, 1990–Oct. 30, 1995   The Hon. Willard Z. Estey
Oct. 27, 1996–June 10, 2003   John E. Cleghorn
Sept. 1, 2003–present   The Hon. Robert (Bob) Rae